The Doctor Will See You Now

DR AMIR KHAN

The Doctor Will See You Now

The high and lows of my
life as an NHS GP

EBURY
PRESS

3 5 7 9 10 8 6 4

Ebury Press, an imprint of Ebury Publishing
20 Vauxhall Bridge Road
London SW1V 2SA

Ebury Press is part of the Penguin Random House group of companies
whose addresses can be found at global.penguinrandomhouse.com

Penguin
Random House
UK

First published by Ebury Press in 2020

www.penguin.co.uk

A CIP catalogue record for this book is available from the British Library

ISBN 9781529107401

Typeset in 11.5/16 pt ITC Galliard Pro
by Integra Software Services Pvt. Ltd, Pondicherry

Printed and bound in Great Britain by Clays Ltd, Elcograf S.p.A.

The events described in this book are based on the experiences and recollections of the author. To preserve patient confidentiality and the privacy of colleagues, names and other identifying features have been changed. The anecdotes described are not based on any one specific individual but rather a selection of composite characters drawing on the various experiences of the author, during his time working in numerous different medical practices and placements. Although a character has been given a name, such as 'Percy', this is for narrative flow rather than because it represents just one person. Any similarities are purely coincidental. This is because this is not a book about the individuals described but about what we can learn from them and how they shape our approach as medical practitioners to our patients and, as readers, to each other.

To all my colleagues in the NHS

Contents

Introduction————————————————————————— 1

Chapter One—————————————————————————— 7

Chapter Two————————————————————————— 25

Chapter Three————————————————————————— 38

Chapter Four————————————————————————— 46

Chapter Five—————————————————————————60

Chapter Six——————————————————————————71

Chapter Seven———————————————————————— 87

Chapter Eight————————————————————————106

Chapter Nine————————————————————————— 126

Chapter Ten—————————————————————————— 142

Chapter Eleven———————————————————————— 155

Chapter Twelve———————————————————————— 162

Chapter Thirteen——————————————————————— 177

Chapter Fourteen——————————————————————— 188

Chapter Fifteen———————————————————————— 209

Contents

Chapter Sixteen—————————————————————— 226

Chapter Seventeen———————————————————— 249

Epilogue———————————————————————————— 256

Acknowledgements——————————————————————261

Introduction

It was the bank holiday weekend and the sun was shining. Sunday afternoon made for the perfect opportunity to go to the garden centre and buy some bedding plants to fill some of the gaps in his garden.

It was busy when he arrived – everyone had obviously had the same idea – so he had to park a fair distance away. But it didn't matter, he didn't mind the walk. There were lots of people wandering around with trolleys filled with plants and ornaments; the coffee shop was brimming with customers ordering cakes and teas.

He followed the signs to the bedding plant area, his empty trolley ready to be filled. The pansies looked good but perhaps he should go for a perennial instead? That way he wouldn't have to fill the gaps again next year. It was a rather nice predicament to be in. He savoured the moment.

'Hi, mate. You're that doctor, aren't you?' A voice cut through his thoughts.

He looked up. A man in his seventies stood there, waiting patiently for an answer.

'Sorry?' he said, taking a minute to come out of his daze.

'I know you, you're that doctor,' the man repeated.

'Yes,' he said, trying to remember if he had ever met this man before. No, definitely not. 'Nice to meet you.' He extended his hand to greet him.

The man ignored his offer of a handshake and instead started unbuttoning his trousers. 'Mate, you wouldn't mind having a look at this, would you? I've been trying to see my own GP for weeks but can't get an appointment.' He pulled down his trousers, accidentally bringing his underpants down with them. He quickly tried to pull them back up again but it was too late, the doctor had already seen too much.

A few other shoppers were starting to give the two of them funny looks. The woman next to them, who was also considering the delphiniums, hurriedly pushed her trolley away.

'I've had this rash in my groin now for nearly a month. It's incredibly itchy and sore. What do you think it is, doc?' the man asked the doctor.

'Shall we go somewhere more private?' the doctor said, acutely aware of the stares from passers-by.

'It's all right, doc. I'm sure you see this kind of thing all the time.' The man wasn't going anywhere without an answer.

The rash did look angry and had clearly been scratched, as there were areas that were bleeding. The doctor was about to say something when a lady wearing the garden centre uniform appeared.

'You have to pull your trousers up immediately,' she said, sharply. 'This is a garden centre for families.' She gave them both a disgusted look.

'It's all right, love,' the man said. 'This man's a doctor. This is a medical problem.' He pointed at his groin. 'Nothing dodgy going on, don't worry.'

'I don't care if he is the Sultan of Brunei; if you don't pull your trousers up now, I'll call security,' she said.

The doctor quickly interjected, desperate to put an end to this scene. 'You can pull up your trousers, I think I know what the rash is.'

The man pulled up his trousers. 'See, I told you: doctor,' he said smugly to the staff member. She rolled her eyes and walked off. 'So what is it, doc?'

'Probably a fungal rash from sweating into your groin. You should be able to buy an antifungal cream from most pharmacies.'

'Cheers, doc,' the man said, wheeling his trolley off.

The doctor couldn't stay in the garden centre a minute longer. He could still feel the eyes of the other shoppers on him. He dumped his empty trolley and made his way hastily to the car.

This was me, on a Sunday afternoon at the garden centre. Full groin rash just waving around in my face. I now go to a different place to buy my perennials.

This year will mark my fifteen-year anniversary of becoming a doctor and my ten-year anniversary of being a full-time GP, and when I say 'full-time' I mean FULL-TIME. Being a doctor is one of those jobs where you simultaneously want to shout it from the rooftops but at the same time don't want anyone to know in case they tell you their entire medical history, usually in the middle of a dancefloor while doing the 'Gangnam Style' routine.

I have been in one of those situations on a plane when the announcement for a doctor goes out and you pause in the hope there might be another medical practitioner aboard. There wasn't. A man had collapsed while coming out of the bathroom. I was asked whether the plane needed diverting to the nearest airport. The question came with pointed looks from nearby passengers. Luckily the man had only fainted but I had to carry out a full examination while he lay on the floor in the aisle. People kept stepping over the two of us to use the lavatory. I wasn't upgraded to business class for my efforts.

Being a GP is also one of those jobs that everybody knows but nobody finds sexy. People are constantly asking me why I didn't choose to specialise in something. Or, in the case of all my relatives, why I didn't want to become a cardiothoracic surgeon like my cousin, Arif. Everybody loves Arif. He had six marriage offers after he finished his surgical training. I only had one; I think it was a pity offer. My mum thought I should take it.

'I'm not expecting any more,' she said.

'I'll sort myself out, thanks, Mum,' I told her.

I mean, I get it – he can perform a heart transplant; that's sexy. But I am brilliant at testing a urine sample or feeling a prostate. There must be someone out there who finds *that* sexy. I keep trying to tell my family that I specialise in EVERYTHING. They don't buy it.

Despite that, being a GP really does give you an 'access all areas' card to people's lives. We are a trusted member of a community; the person you can talk to in confidence about anything. We are there for the highest of highs and the lowest of lows. We are the first medical professional to see a woman when she is pregnant or a man when he wants the snip. When a child is unwell, it's us that the parents will ring for help before anyone else. But it doesn't stop there. GPs will come out and see your loved ones if they are dying at home or are feeling so low they want to kill themselves. We might be the only person you ever tell about that one-night stand before we prescribe you the morning-after pill.

And we do all of this in ten minutes (well, kind of).

Beat that, Arif.

*

Introduction

In this book, I will bring you ten years' worth of stories from the frontline of the NHS, and give you an insight into the daily life of an inner-city GP in modern Britain. All names and medical details have been changed to protect patient anonymity, and no one story is based on any individual case; they are a reflection on my experiences working in the medical field.

Ten years is a relatively short time to spend being a GP, but a lot has changed in that period. The profession has gone from its golden years where there was stiff competition for jobs to crisis point. It is difficult now to watch the news or open a paper without seeing something about another GP practice closing down due to not being able to recruit enough doctors. Worse, there are increasingly alarming stories of doctors working in primary care killing themselves due to the pressure and responsibility that comes with being a GP.

Modern-day general practice involves more paperwork and many more meetings than in the past, and the patients' issues are getting far more complex. But the personal interaction between a doctor and their patient remains at the centre of the role – and is what keeps me drawn to the profession. I may only get ten minutes with a person, and often that is not nearly enough, but I can make it count. I can listen, empathise and help the individual who has come to see me. That has not changed in all the years general practice has been around.

So, it may be an overworked and undervalued line of work, but all of these encounters have led to some of the most heartwarming and heartbreaking stories in my life, and that makes it one of the best jobs in the world.

Welcome to my surgery.

Chapter One

My first day as a fully qualified GP. I had debated over whether to wear a tie or not – I wanted to make a good first impression but didn't want to commit to something I couldn't sustain in the long term. In the end I decided against the tie and went for a freshly ironed pale blue shirt and grey trousers. One of the nurses I used to work with once advised me against wearing a white shirt on the first day of any job.

'You want them to think you've made an effort but haven't peaked,' she told me. 'Blue is a good colour to start with and then there is room to move forward as time goes on. If you start with white, there is nowhere to go from there.' For some reason those words played in my head that morning. I put on my blue shirt.

I was nervous; it was a new practice, in a new area. I had completed my three years of GP training just three days ago. Many of my peers had opted to take a few weeks off before jumping into work but, to be honest, I couldn't afford to. University had been expensive and junior doctors don't get paid very much.

I pulled into the car park. There was a special area that said 'Doctors' Parking' and was made up of five bays. Was I allowed to park here? I didn't want to park in someone else's space, but I *was* a doctor and I did work here. I grappled with it in my mind for a few moments. No, I thought, I couldn't in case it meant one of the other doctors grumbled at me for having taken their space. I did a quick turn around and parked in the patients' car park.

I stared at the building. It looked so different to my training practice. I took a deep breath and grabbed the tin of biscuits I had got from Sainsbury's the night before. I was going to give them to the receptionists; it was always good to get them onside. I got out of the car and headed towards the front door. There was a queue of patients waiting for the door to open. Did I just push past them to the front? How was I going to get in anyway? I didn't have the key. I decided to wait at the back of the line until the doors opened.

The man ahead of me turned to look at me.

'You're a bit dressed up, aren't ya?' he said, then started with a coughing fit. 'It's my emphysema, this weather flares it up.' He took out an inhaler from his pocket and tried taking a puff which set his coughing off again. Delving into his top pocket, he pulled out a handkerchief and summoned up a loud hack which sent a large piece of green phlegm hurtling into the centre of it. He inspected the phlegm for a beat longer than was needed, then, seemingly satisfied, folded the handkerchief up and placed it back in his pocket. 'What are you here for?'

'Oh, I work here now,' I said nervously. 'First day today.'

'Work here? Well, I hope you can do something about the bloody appointment system. It's easier to get an appointment with the Queen than it is to see a doctor.'

Before I had time to answer, one of the receptionists appeared in the window of the door, opening it and allowing everyone to make their way inside. I rushed past everyone to catch her up.

'Hi, I'm Amir, the new GP,' I said.

'Hetty. Don't you know about the staff entrance round the back?' she said. 'Come on, I'll show you.'

Hetty looked to be in her mid-forties and was rather dressed up for work, I thought. She seemed to make the dreary receptionists' uniform work for her. Her blonde hair was set in a large beehive and she wore red lipstick and a bit too much blusher. She looked like she was entering a beauty pageant rather than booking appointments for our patients.

Hetty showed me the code for the door where the staff entered from and I jotted it down in my brand-new notepad. I had always wanted to be one of those people who carried around meticulously organised notepads or Filofaxes. As a rule, I was hopelessly disorganised and relied on other people to remind me of where I needed to be and when. But not this time. This was a new chapter and I was going to iron my shirts and make notes in my fancy new notebook and I would not lose it, not ever. Closing the pad, I placed it carefully into my new satchel.

I surrendered my tin of biscuits over as I said hello to the other receptionists.

'You know how to make a good first impression, Amir, I'll give you that,' Hetty said. 'But if you really want to impress us, you better get started on your list. Your first patient is already here.'

Hetty showed me to my room and then left. I had a moment of panic as I sat alone unpacking my things. Being a GP is very different to working in a hospital. People assume it is easier and that patients come in with minor ailments that can be seen and sorted in the allocated ten minutes. The truth is very different. In hospital you are part of a team of clinicians investigating and diagnosing a patient's symptoms. When patients are admitted to a hospital ward, they have usually been seen by a junior doctor who takes a thorough history and orders an array of investigations, which generally come back on the same day. The patient is then reviewed by a more senior member of the team with the results to hand and a management plan is put into place. If they require further investigations or treatment, they are usually kept on the ward under the close eye of the ward staff until they get them done, all the while being reviewed by the doctors on a daily basis. If they are deemed well enough to go home, they are often told to see their GP if things get any worse. It is a system that works, quite rightly, in favour of patient safety. Only patients with the most minor of presentations are sent home without some sort of diagnostic investigation or follow-up.

It is different in general practice, as the pendulum swings very much towards relying on the doctor's clinical judgement. The results of any investigations we order often take days or weeks to come back to us, which means we have ten minutes to talk to, examine, diagnose and manage each patient. And now that I was no longer a GP trainee, I wouldn't even have my senior GP colleagues to review the patients I saw. I tried to swallow the panic that was rising in my throat. I had been trained to do this, I was going to be fine.

I called in my first patient, an 81-year-old man called Derek Shoesmith. I'd had a brief look through his notes before calling him in. Mr Shoesmith had a history of diabetes, high blood pressure and arthritis.

'Hello, Mr Shoesmith. I'm Dr Khan, how can I help?' I said a bit more cheerfully than I had meant to. *Tone it down, Amir*, I thought.

Mr Shoesmith was wearing a brown tweed jacket and a blue shirt that was tucked into his trousers. He shuffled rather than walked, and was propped up by a stick which didn't look like it would hold him if he leaned too far one way. He wore a grey flat cap which he took off as he sat down. 'I've come about my cough,' he said. 'I think I may have a chest infection.'

Chapter 1

'Okay, tell me a bit more about your cough.' I leaned forward in my chair. A cough was something I could handle, something straightforward to ease me into my first day.

'Well, it started a few days ago, I'm bringing up some phlegm with it.'

'Any chest pain or shortness of breath?' I ventured. I was getting into my stride now.

'I have been a bit short of breath, usually when I go upstairs.'

'Ah, I see. Have you ever noticed any blood in that phlegm you've been coughing up?'

'No, it's mainly white with a tinge of green.'

'Thanks, Mr Shoesmith. Do you mind if I have a listen to your chest?'

'That's what I'm here for,' he said, taking off his jacket. I went behind him and lifted up his shirt, about to put my stethoscope on the back of his chest. As I did so, I noticed a bruise on the right side of his ribs. I touched it, making him recoil and pull down his shirt.

'Mr Shoesmith, where did you get that bruise from?' I asked.

He shifted slightly in his chair, pulling at a loose thread on the flat cap he was holding. 'It's nothing. I just fell when I was out in the garden.'

'It looks very sore. When did it happen?'

'Just last week. I didn't want to bother the doctors about it. It really isn't anything to worry about, it's already starting to feel better.'

'Can I take another look at it? I need to listen to your chest anyway.' Mr Shoesmith looked at me reluctantly before lifting up his shirt again. I felt over the bruise with my fingers, pressing on the rib underneath. Mr Shoesmith winced each time. 'I'm sorry if I'm hurting you,' I said. 'I just want to see if the rib underneath is broken.' I finished off by listening to his chest, asking him to take deep breaths, something he clearly found uncomfortable to do. There did seem to be an infection just under the bruised area, which wasn't unusual for elderly people with rib injuries. The pain restricted them from taking full breaths, which meant air didn't move as freely in and out of lungs, allowing bacteria to colonise the area.

I sat in my chair, looking at my patient. Clinicians have what I now call a 'Spidey Sense', something that tingles when things don't quite add up. Often it goes off when you come across a patient who needs urgent treatment; other times it picks up subtler irregularities. Mine was tingling now.

'Mr Shoesmith, you certainly sound like you have a bit of infection brewing in your chest. Nothing that some antibiotics won't clear up. But I am more worried about that bruise; it looks like you may have broken a rib.'

'Oh no, I'm sure it's not as serious as all that,' he countered, tucking his shirt back in protectively.

'Tell me again how it happened?' I said.

'I can't really remember now. I must have knocked it on something, the corner of a table perhaps.'

Now my Spidey Sense was in full alarm mode. 'Mr Shoesmith, I am not trying to catch you out or anything, but you just told me you thought you did it falling in the garden.'

'I can't remember, it was a few days ago.' He was looking down at his cap, pulling again at the loose thread. The fingers on his right hand were stained from smoking, and a scar from a healing scratch wound ran from the back of his hand and disappeared up his sleeve.

'That looks like a nasty scratch, Mr Shoesmith,' I said, gesturing at his hand. 'Do you mind me asking how you got that?'

Chapter 1

I had to be careful; I wanted to sound like a concerned doctor and not an enquiring police officer. It was a fine line. He immediately put his left hand over the scratch.

'Probably in the garden again,' he said quietly.

I took a moment. I had only known Derek Shoesmith for a few minutes. If there was something he wasn't telling me I would have to get him to trust me first.

'Mr Shoesmith, I'm conscious we haven't met before. Do you mind telling me who you live at home with?' The change of tack caught him off guard and he looked up.

'My wife, June,' he said, sounding relieved to be in more comfortable territory.

'Do you have any children?'

'Yes, two boys. One works with computers in Canada, the other lives in London.'

'Do you get to see them much?'

'They do visit, usually once a year. They have their own lives, and their work and families keep them busy.'

'And your wife, June, is she well?' I asked.

That seemed to unsettle him. 'We manage,' he said, shifting in his chair. 'Dr Khan, I would like it if you could give me my prescription now. I don't want to take up any more of your time.'

I knew the consultation had come to an end. Mr Shoesmith was already buttoning up his coat and putting on his hat.

'I hope you don't mind me asking you those questions, Mr Shoesmith. It's my first day, you see, and I just want to get to know my patients,' I lied, printing off his prescription.

'I understand,' he said curtly. 'If I could just have my prescription.' He took the piece of paper.

'Do come back if your cough doesn't improve,' I said as he shuffled towards the door.

'Thank you, Dr Khan. I will.' He struggled with the weight of the door, and I got up to help him. 'I can manage,' he said. I sat back down and watched him leave.

I was annoyed with myself. I hadn't played that right at all and as a result Mr Shoesmith hadn't disclosed the causes for his injuries. I could hear my GP trainer's voice in my head. Every GP trainee has their own individual GP mentor called a GP trainer. That term always reminds me of the circus, like I was an elephant or lion that needed a trainer in order to perform. Mine used to say, 'The thing about general practice is that you don't have to solve everything in the first ten minutes. Think of some consultations as a jumping-off point; you can pick up where you left off in the next consultation. It's a marathon not a sprint.'

I despised it when people said 'it's a marathon not a sprint'.

I had realised by that point in my life that I wasn't a very patient man. I wanted to know the answers to everything at once. I didn't do well with mystery or suspense, or 'managing uncertainty', which is what they called it in the profession. I would have to learn.

The rest of the morning seemed to fly by. I called each patient in with a quiet trepidation, but once they were in I found my stride and managed well. I was beginning to believe I was getting the hang of things when a message from Hetty popped up on my screen. Emergency in room six!

I stared at it. Perhaps it was a mistake and not meant for me. There were at least two other GPs in the building. Surely they would be better equipped to deal with whatever was happening? I thought briefly about dismissing it and calling in my next patient. I couldn't do it. I grabbed my stethoscope and made my way to room six.

The room was being used by Kathryn Connor, one of the advanced nurse practitioners. Nurse practitioners are registered nurses who have done further training and are qualified to diagnose and manage acute and undifferentiated medical problems. Hetty was in there too. I knew immediately that things couldn't be too good because Hetty's perfect beehive was coming loose. Strands of wild blonde hair were flailing about.

'Who's this?' Kathryn Connor said to Hetty.

'Amir, one of the new doctors,' Hetty said.

Kathryn was standing by the examination couch where a female patient in her early twenties lay. The patient didn't look well as she writhed around on her back.

'This is Fliss, she is nineteen and presented with abdominal pain. It started last night and has got worse this morning,' Kathryn said as I made my way over to the couch. Fliss was a large lady, probably weighing about eighteen stone, and the couch wasn't very wide so Kathryn was holding on to her to stop her falling off.

'Any bowel or urinary symptoms?' I asked. Kathryn shook her head.

'Ahhhhhhhhh!' Fliss cried out, holding on to her belly.

'Kathryn, is she pregnant?' I said, horrified.

'No, I am *not* pregnant!' Fliss shouted from behind Kathryn.

'She says her last period was only a few days ago,' Kathryn said, 'but I'm not so sure.'

Fliss let out a scream again. Something about her face didn't seem quite right: only half of it was moving when she screamed. Kathryn read my mind.

'She has a Bell's palsy. Diagnosed a few weeks ago, still recovering,' she said.

A Bell's palsy is a facial paralysis that affects one side of the face only, generally caused by a viral infection. Although nothing serious, it can take months to resolve. Unfortunately for Fliss, it meant that every time she cried out, only half of her face worked.

'Hi, Fliss, I am Dr Khan. Do you mind if I have a feel of your tummy?' Fliss nodded. I lifted up her dress and felt her abdomen. It was immediately clear what was going on. I turned to Hetty.

'Hetty, I need sterile gloves and could you bring in the crash trolley?' She nodded and left to get some from the nurses' room. 'Fliss, tell me why you don't think you could be pregnant?'

'I'm not pregnant,' she said again. 'Me and my boyfriend are really careful. And I just had a period. Also, I did a pregnancy test last night and it was negative.' She held on to her tummy and screamed again. 'What's wrong with me?' she begged, sounding scared.

'When you say careful, what kind of contraception are you using?' I asked, hand still on her belly.

Half of Fliss's face looked sheepish. 'Sometimes we use condoms,' she said.

'And the other times?' I asked. Kathryn rolled her eyes. Clearly this was a conversation she had already had with her.

'The withdrawal technique,' Fliss said quietly.

Wow, okay, I thought. Fliss gave another cry and this time I definitely felt her abdomen contract.

'I'm afraid, Fliss, the withdrawal technique isn't very reliable and it looks like a few of your partner's swimmers managed to escape before he withdrew,' I said. Hetty had returned with the gloves and the emergency trolley. 'Hetty, can you call for an ambulance? Tell them I think we have a patient in labour, blue light please.' Hetty disappeared again.

I took a deep breath. I had done a six-month placement in obstetrics and gynaecology as part of my GP training and had been present at several births on the labour ward. But I hadn't actually delivered a baby myself. I was usually shoved to one side by the midwives who managed these things with ease and I was just asked to stitch up any tears afterwards.

I needed to know how far along this labour was, and whether we had time to get Fliss to hospital or not.

'Fliss, I think you may be in labour. I need to do an internal examination to see how far along you are,' I said.

'No, no, no, I can't be pregnant. I just can't be.' Poor Fliss was tearing up.

I felt sorry for her: she had come to see Kathryn about some tummy pain and would likely leave with a baby. Even though she had been a little naïve about her methods of contraception, she looked very vulnerable there on the couch with no partner present. The hormone pregnancy tests look for are only present in the early part of pregnancy, so her test would have been negative. As for her recent period, it wasn't uncommon for some women to have a small bleed or 'show' a few days before labour.

'Fliss, is it okay for me to examine you now?' I asked again. She nodded.

I felt for the cervix. I wasn't surprised to find it dilated to an estimation of seven centimetres. I could feel the top of baby's head.

'Kathryn, she's about seven centimetres. Can you help her with her breathing?' I was being sexist; I assumed Kathryn had children of her own and that she could remember the breathing exercises she had done during the birth of her own children. I was starting to feel out of my depth. I was desperate for the ambulance crew to arrive – I estimated the baby would come in the next couple of hours but really it could come anytime, and I wasn't sure what I would do if things got complicated.

'Fliss, I know this is not what you want to hear. But you are in labour and are going to have a baby. I am hoping the ambulance will arrive and get you to the hospital in time, but if that doesn't happen, you will be perfectly safe here,' I lied. Inside, I was panicking. This had disaster written all over it: we were simply not equipped to deliver babies in general practice, and even less equipped to deal with any complications of labour. 'Is there anyone we should call?'

'My boyfriend Malcolm. He'll be at work, but please can you call him?' I rummaged through Fliss's handbag and found her mobile phone. She dialled Malcolm's number. I was hoping she would tell him herself, but she shoved the phone back into my hands.

'Oh hello, is that Malcolm?' I said. 'This is Dr Khan from the doctors' surgery.'

'What's wrong? Is it Fliss?' Malcolm replied.

'I think you should probably come to the surgery, as we are having to admit Fliss to the hospital. It's urgent.' I just couldn't tell him about the baby on the phone; that was something that warranted a face-to-face discussion. Preferably between him and Fliss. Malcolm said he would make his way over and hung up.

'Amir, the contractions are getting closer together,' Kathryn said, who had been brilliant so far in supporting Fliss as I tried to stay calm. It was too early to examine Fliss again, but I knew things were progressing.

There was a knock on the door. Hetty came back in; her hair had miraculously returned to its perfect state and her lipstick looked as though it had been reapplied. She was followed by two paramedics. Thank God.

I gave them a brief summary of events. They decided the best thing to do was to get Fliss into a chair and take her straight to the labour ward. She had a contraction just before they moved her. Both looked at me.

'Bell's palsy,' I said. A look of relief passed over their faces, but it was nothing compared to the look of relief that passed over my face as they wheeled Fliss out.

'Not how you expected to meet the new doctor,' I said to Kathryn, trying to sound confident and assured. I was feeling neither.

'No, but it could have been worse. You might have had to deliver that baby,' Kathryn said as we tidied up. Something told me that Kathryn knew just how out of my depth I had been. 'Besides, I am more interested in what you're going to say to Malcolm when he arrives.'

I had forgotten about poor Malcolm, who was making his way to the surgery. I asked Hetty to ring him and for him to meet Fliss at the hospital. I imagined he would smell a rat when he was directed to go to the labour ward.

Somehow I managed to get through the rest of my first day. As I tidied up my desk and turned off my computer, still turning over the events of the previous hours, the words of my GP trainer echoed again in my head, now sounding rather hollow. Fliss's situation, after all, had been the very definition of a sprint not a marathon.

My adrenaline was still running high when I got home that night. But it wasn't the incident with Fliss that was occupying my thoughts, it was Mr Shoesmith. I felt I had left that consultation unfinished, and I wasn't sure how I was going to get a second chance at it. I could ring him up next week to see if he had recovered from his chest infection, but then if he wouldn't open up to me in person, he was even less likely to do so on the phone. I couldn't see a way to approach him without it sounding like an interrogation. Maybe I was being silly, perhaps he had just injured himself in the garden. I decided I was reading too much into it and went to bed.

I didn't have to wait too long to solve the Shoesmith Mystery. A few weeks later, I was assigned a home visit to see Mrs Shoesmith. I recognised the name immediately. The note made by the receptionists said Mr Shoesmith had rung up worried his wife had a urinary tract infection, and had requested a home visit as she was too unwell to come to the surgery.

Mr Shoesmith let me in when I arrived. The house was a small bungalow. He led me into the living room and said he would fetch his wife who was upstairs. I stood looking around. The carpet had a floral pattern on it and in the centre of the room there was a small wooden coffee table with an ashtray on top that looked well used. Two large armchairs faced towards an old-looking television set. There were photos of grandchildren on a chest of drawers on one side of the room, and net curtains dappling the sunlight on the other.

'This is the doctor, love,' Mr Shoesmith said as he walked his wife in.

June Shoesmith was wearing a dark green blouse, grey skirt and black tights. On her feet were pink fluffy slippers that looked out of place on her. I presumed they had been a gift bought for her by someone else.

'Is he here to see the boys?' June asked, looking at me then at her husband.

'No, he is here to see you. You haven't been too well the last couple of days.'

'Haven't I?' June replied.

'Hi, Mrs Shoesmith. My name is Dr Khan. I wonder if we can have a chat.' I gestured for her to sit down on one of the armchairs.

Chapter 1

'I don't see why, I am feeling perfectly fine,' June said as she took a seat. I crouched down beside her.

'Your husband was worried you may have an infection in your waterworks?' I said gently.

'No, I don't think I have. Are you from the post office?' she said, looking at her husband now rather than me.

'She has had a few accidents this week, doctor. It's not like her,' Mr Shoesmith offered.

'Doctor, I didn't recognise you there. How are your children?' Mrs Shoesmith asked, looking closely at me, but mistaking me for someone else.

I had read June's notes before coming out. It wasn't unusual for elderly people to be confused if they had an infection but there had been no mention of any other memory impairment. I asked June a few more questions, checked her pulse, felt her abdomen and listened to her chest. Everything was normal. 'I think one of the boys may have hurt his knee, it's good you came. I'll just go and get him,' she said when I'd finished. She got up and made her way back into the hallway.

'Mr Shoesmith, do you mind if we talk?' I said before he had chance to follow her out. He sighed and sat down. This time, I took the other armchair. 'June may have a urine infection, Mr Shoesmith, but she does seem more confused than I was expecting.' Mr Shoesmith looked straight ahead at the blank television screen. 'How long has she been confused for?'

'She wet herself a few times this week, Dr Khan. I think that has made things worse,' he replied.

'Did she manage to clean herself up or did you have to help?' I asked.

'I had to do it,' he replied.

'Did she know she had done it?' I asked. He shook his head. 'What else do you have to do for her?' He didn't answer. 'Mr Shoesmith, we may be able to help.'

He sighed. 'I have to dress her in the morning. Wash her, too. She can't do it on her own any more.'

'How did you get that bruise on your back when I saw you last time?'

'I slipped in the bathroom when I was washing her, hit it on the corner of the sink. I didn't have my stick with me and the floor was wet,' he said. We both sat in silence for a minute. I was planning my next question carefully.

'Why haven't you mentioned this to anyone before?'

Mr Shoesmith didn't say anything.

'Do your boys know?'

He shook his head.

'She was a wonderful woman you know, Dr Khan. A wonderful wife and a wonderful mother.' Mr Shoesmith stared back at the television. Our images were distorted in the reflection. 'Of course, she isn't that woman any longer.'

'I'm sorry, Mr Shoesmith. It must be difficult looking after her without any help.'

'Have you ever lost someone, Dr Khan?'

I paused, not knowing how much to give away. 'My father died a few years ago.'

'I'm sorry to hear that,' Mr Shoesmith said. 'I lost my wife two years ago. She is here in this house, but it's not her. Sometimes she comes back, just for a minute, but then she is gone again. It's like she has been taken away over and over again.' His voice was flat, devoid of any emotion.

'Mr Shoesmith, there are things we can do to help. Things we can put in place.'

'We promised we wouldn't send each other to nursing homes, if that's what you're suggesting. We know what those places can be like. I promised her that when she first started getting confused, she would worry about it so much. Besides, I couldn't be in this house on my own, we've lived here for over fifty years.' He clasped the top of his walking stick, turning his knuckles white. I could see the mark on his hand again.

'Does she ever get violent?' I asked, nodding to his hand.

'Sometimes at night, when she wakes up and gets out of bed. That's when it's worse, she is so disorientated. She doesn't know who I am during those times. It's not her fault. She gets frightened and doesn't know what she is doing.'

'That must be difficult for you. But you really don't have to care for her on your own. We can help.' I tried to get him to look at me. 'Do you have any friends or neighbours who you have told?'

He shook his head. 'We used to see friends, but since June started becoming poorly we slowly stopped seeing them. I can only leave her for a short period to do the shopping, then I have to come straight home.'

June came back in. 'I can't seem to find the boys. They must be out on their bikes.' She left again.

I explained to Mr Shoesmith that there were lots of different causes of memory impairment in the elderly and persuaded him to let me carry out some blood tests on June. He accepted a referral to the local memory clinic and input from our community matron.

June turned out to have Alzheimer's dementia, and was started on some medication to help slow down its progression. The couple were offered a package of care which involved people coming in twice a day to help June out of bed and get her dressed, returning in the evenings to help get her ready for bed. As time went on this was extended to four visits a day. Two years later, June died at home. I thought about Mr Shoesmith having to go through the feelings of losing his wife for the last time. The couple had been happily married for sixty years. If anyone knew about life being a marathon, not a sprint, it was Mr Shoesmith.

Our practice has a tradition that was set up by one of the receptionists who has long left the surgery. We send condolence cards and a bunch of flowers out to the family members of our patients who have died. The card is signed by the doctor who was most involved in that patient's care. The card came to me on the morning of June's death. I sat at my desk, thinking of the message I would write in it before starting.

Dear Mr Shoesmith

I am sorry for your loss. I am sure June would be pleased you kept your promise to her.

Best wishes
Dr Amir Khan

Chapter Two

Working in healthcare is a tough job. The workload pressures are relentless and there is always a demand that simply cannot be met. However, the staff within the NHS are second to none; most will go out of their way to help patients, often staying late or putting in that extra effort.

At the same time, you are constantly apologising to your patients for running late or for them having to wait weeks to see you.

'Every time we ring, you never have any appointments,' they say.

This is true; it is difficult for patients to get appointments. At our practice, patients have to ring first thing in the morning and wait in a telephone queue which is akin to a lottery system or brave the elements and queue up outside. The same is true for almost every GP surgery up and down the country.

What I want to tell them is that I am there from 7 a.m. every morning and often don't leave until 7 p.m. If they cannot get an appointment, it will be because we are seeing the other patients that are also desperate to see us. We have tried employing more reception staff to answer the phones and even spent a small fortune on employing more clinical staff to help, but the beast is insatiable; the more you feed it the more it wants.

What this system does is almost pit patients against their doctors, as by the time they get seen they are fed up and angry, and that is understandable. Sadly, it is the reception staff who are thought of as the villains in this story, as they are the ones who have to break the news to patients that all the appointments have been given out and that they will now have to try again the next morning. 'Dragons' and 'the Gestapo', they are often called, simply for doing their jobs and getting caught in the crossfire. Poor Hetty is constantly adjusting her beehive after every heated debate with a patient about appointments.

The truth of the matter is that primary care is seriously underfunded, and demand exceeds supply several-fold. No matter what new schemes the government try to force on us, there is only so much lipstick you can put on a pig. And this particular sow already has a full face of make-up.

Instead of saying all this to my irate patients, I just apologise yet again and hope one day I will be making a silk purse.

Because we all feel this pressure, there is a comradeship within the NHS. A sense that we are all in it together, and even though the government can't get it right and the funding will always fall short, we, as the people who work for the NHS, will give it all we have got. The nature of the job means you share some of life's most significant moments with your colleagues, be it the death of a patient you have all been involved in the care of, diagnosing a life-changing medical condition and breaking that news to a patient, or happier occasions such as the birth of a baby. Friendships are forged due to these shared experiences, often with likeminded individuals who want to help people, the same as you.

I am lucky enough to work with some of my best friends. I didn't know them before I started working at the surgery, but over time we have got each other through some the darkest and funniest moments of our lives.

Alison Daniels is one such friend.

The first time I met Alison was over a vaginal examination. I had seen a nineteen-year-old girl who was complaining of vaginal discharge.

'Now any time a patient comes in with discharge from the vagina, we have to ask about their sexual activity,' I said to the patient.

'What *about* my sexual activity?' the girl replied. She was chewing gum, loudly and with an open mouth. I could see it rolling around on her tongue with every chew. It was very distracting.

'Well, are you sexually active?'

'No, what a *rude* question,' she said. 'I am a virgin.' Her thick South Asian accent meant she pronounced it 'wirgin' with a 'w' which I found a bit odd.

'Sorry, I didn't mean to be rude, it's just something we have to ask.'

'Well you don't have to ask *me*. I'm not some kind of slag.' Her chewing was getting louder as she became more irate.

'Of course, I'm not suggesting anything of the sort.' The situation was heading in an uncomfortable direction; I had to get it back on track. 'There are lots of other reasons for vaginal discharge. Would you like me to take a look and a swab? For these kinds of intimate examinations, I do always ask for a nurse to be present as a chaperone.'

She didn't look interested and gave me a simple assent.

Alison was working in the room next door but we hadn't yet been formally introduced. I knocked on her door.

'Hi, Alison, I'm Amir, the new doctor.'

Alison was in her fifties and had one of those reassuringly warm faces, the kind every nurse should have.

She beamed at me. 'Oh, I've heard all about you, Amir. There's already talk about those tight trousers you wear. Bloody hell, they weren't kidding!' she said, looking at me closely. 'I can tell you're circumcised through those trousers!'

'Oh well, yes, they are bit tight,' I said, looking down at my legs, somewhat taken aback by the directness of the conversation. 'I don't suppose you could chaperone me doing a pelvic examination on my patient next door?'

''Course I can, my love.' She got up and we returned to my room together.

'Now then, my love, my name is Alison and I am one of the nurse practitioners,' she said, manoeuvring the patient into the right position for me to do the exam and take a swab.

As I examined the girl, I noticed the clear discharge the patient had been complaining about. I had seen this many times before and knew exactly what it was: chlamydia. I explained what I was doing and completed my examination.

The patient got dressed and sat down.

'I know you said you weren't sexually active, but I just want to make sure, as one of the things I am testing for will be sexually transmitted diseases,' I said. Alison was still in the room.

'No, I've told you before, I'm a wirgin. You calling me a liar?' she said, a bit more loudly this time.

'Of course not,' I said hurriedly. 'I'm sorry but I just had to check. We'll send the swabs to the lab and ring you in the next few days with the results.'

The patient got up and walked out.

'Amir, if that patient is a virgin then I am Mary Queen of Scots,' Alison said. 'That girl's got the clap.'

Chapter 2

'Yep I know, but the proof will be in the pudding,' I said, labelling the swab and placing it carefully into a bag.

That was the beginning of our friendship.

A few days later the swab came back positive for chlamydia. Normally, I would phone up a patient with a positive chlamydia result and make them an appointment at the sexual health clinic, but not this time. This time, I wanted to deliver the news in person.

'Now look,' I said when the girl turned back up at our practice as requested, 'we have the results back from the swab and it does show an infection. You told me last time that you had never had sex, is that statement still true?'

'Yes,' she said, but this time not as forcefully. 'Why?'

'Okay, well, I am sorry to be the one to have to tell you this, but the swab confirms you have chlamydia.'

There was a moment of silence.

'That BASTARD!' she shouted, pulling out her phone and dialling a number. *'I'll fucking kill him.'*

I gave her the contact for the sexual health clinic as she left the room screeching into her phone. It seemed that mine and Alison's instinct had been right, after all – she might have been a wirgin but she certainly wasn't a virgin.

Since that first encounter, Alison and I have been firm friends. We have been on holiday together and got each other through some of the most difficult times in our lives. She was the first person to come and visit me in my new home and, instead of sitting down expecting a cup of tea, she put on a pair of Marigolds and helped me clean it from top to bottom.

When we were both feeling the pressure of our workload getting to us, we decided to book on to a 'mindfulness' course.

Neither of us really knew much about mindfulness, but one of our GPs had been on it before and said it really helped her focus and reduce her stress levels. Also, it was a day off work and it was free. I picked Alison up from her home and drove to the course. It was to be held in a community centre in a small village in Yorkshire.

'Don't worry, Alison, if it's shit we'll make our excuses and go for a nice lunch instead,' I said as we drove up to the venue.

As usual, we were late. We arrived into the hall where the chairs were arranged in a circle. Most were already full but we found two together. The class had already begun. There was a lady in the middle of the circle giving out instructions in soft tones. She looked like she had never had a day of stress in her life. Her shiny brown hair was tied back in a high ponytail and her smooth skin positively glowed. She wore black leggings and a bright pink T-shirt which showed off her perfect abs. *If this is what mindfulness makes you look like, then count me in,* I thought. Alison and I would have perfect abs and shiny new hair by the end of the day.

'Raise your arms high, then move them outwards in a circle,' she said. 'Don't forget to keep moving your heels up and down. Just because you are in a chair doesn't mean you should keep your feet still.'

Everyone obeyed, and they all seemed to know what to do. Alison and I looked a bit clumsy following these instructions.

After five minutes of arm raising, shoulder moving and leg extensions, I turned to Alison.

'God, Alison, this mindfulness is not at all what I had in mind,' I said, panting. My hair felt sweaty and matted rather than shiny and glowing.

'Me neither,' Alison puffed. 'I'm knackered. I thought this was supposed to be relaxing?'

Chapter 2

'Maybe it's just the warm-up? You know, the "getting to know everyone" part before the real class begins,' I replied.

Alison turned round to the lady sitting in the chair next to her, still lifting her arms up and down.

'Excuse me, love, is mindfulness always this much hard work?'

'Mindfulness? No, this is "chairobics". Mindfulness is in the room next door.'

Alison and I left promptly after that. We gave up on the idea of mindfulness and went for a pub lunch instead. To be honest, I think we were even more stressed at the end of that day than we were at the beginning.

One morning much later, after eight years of friendship and working together, Alison came into my room.

'Amir, I don't want you to get upset but I have something to tell you,' she said calmly. I didn't like the tone of this opening statement; it sounded ominous. When someone tells you not to get upset before they tell you something, clearly it is going to be upsetting news.

As a doctor, you live in constant fear that something you have done has resulted in the death or harm of a patient. Although you know this is an irrational fear, it's very difficult to shake it. So whenever a conversation starts like this, that's where your mind goes. Was Alison coming to tell me I had accidentally killed someone?

We have something at our practice that Alison and I refer to as the 'Deceased List'. We look after lots of elderly and very unwell patients, and if any of them die the reception staff send round a message stating that a patient has died and who the last person to see them was. This is the Deceased List. More often than not, it is an expected death and the GP has done everything correctly. Nevertheless, you live in fear of your name being on that list next to a deceased patient.

Oh God, I had a mortgage to pay, how could I do that if I was about to get struck off? I would be homeless. What would I do if I wasn't a doctor? My mum would *kill* me.

'Okay, I promise not to get upset,' I said calmly, as if none of these thoughts were in my head. *Professional, stay professional,* I thought.

My self-centred panicking was instantly silenced by what Alison said next. 'I went to see my doctor yesterday because I had some bleeding "down below" and he has referred me urgently to see a gynaecologist,' she said quietly. I could see tears welling up in Alison's eyes.

Alison had been through the menopause. She wasn't supposed to bleed any more. I knew – and she knew – that if a patient comes in with bleeding after the menopause there is a chance it could be cancer of the womb.

'Oh Alison, I am so sorry. How are you feeling?' I said.

'I feel fine, but it's been more than once so I thought I better get it checked out.' Alison paused. 'I think Marcus is worried.' Marcus is Alison's husband, and the senior GP partner at our practice.

Medical professionals are the worst for getting medical help. We all know that even a single episode of postmenopausal bleeding warrants urgent investigation. It was typical that Alison had waited for it to happen more than once. We can use our busy schedules as an excuse, or that it's hard for us to admit we need help, but sometimes it's because we know how serious these things can be more than anyone and we just don't want to be confronted with the truth.

Chapter 2

'When is your appointment with the gynaecologist?'

'Next Tuesday,' she replied.

'Is Marcus going with you?' I asked.

'He can't, he is away teaching on a course that he can't get out of.'

'Well, someone needs to go with you. You can't go on your own.'

'Don't be silly, of course I can go on my own. It will be fine,' Alison said unconvincingly.

I thought about what I was doing next Tuesday. It was Eid.

Eid is a Muslim religious festival, and I had booked the day off work. It is always a hectic day; we all gather at my mum's house for a big family lunch and there is lots of gift giving. Well, actually we give cold hard cash to each other, the best gift of all. It's exactly how I imagine Christmas is, except with more twenty-pound notes. The kids really enjoy it and the whole day is spent welcoming visiting guests to the house, offering food for each one again and again and again.

My mum is strict about Eid; her family isn't allowed to work during it. We have to be present at the house all day. It's the one day she insists we are all together.

'I can come with you,' I said.

'Only if you're sure?' Alison seemed relieved.

'I'm sure. I'll meet you at the hospital.'

Eid was as busy as expected. Mum cooked up a feast, we had an endless number of visitors and there were the usual obligatory family fall-outs that always happen at large get-togethers.

At three o'clock I made my excuses amid the chaos and drove up to the hospital.

Alison was already there. I waved at her as I entered. She smiled as she saw me then a look of surprise came over her face when she saw what I was wearing.

Eid is the *only* day of the year when I wear traditional Asian clothes. They are called shalwaar kameez. Basically they're a pair of large billowing cotton trousers, not dissimilar to what you would imagine Aladdin to be wearing, and a long loose shirt that comes down below my knees. I was also wearing silver shoes that curled up at the end, again a bit like what you would expect Aladdin to wear. In the hubbub at my mum's house, I had completely forgotten to change.

'Nice outfit,' Alison said.

'I can get one in Marcus's size if you want?' I said.

'I think I'll give that a miss!' Alison replied.

We waited to be called in. It was weird being on the other side, being a patient. We had no control, we just had to wait until the doctor was ready to see us.

Eventually, our turn came.

'Alison Daniels?' the receptionist called.

We got up and were led into the consulting room. 'The doctor will be with you in a few minutes,' the receptionist said as she left.

'Are you nervous, Alison?' I asked.

'Yes, I think I am. I just keep worrying about Marcus. My kids will be okay, they're grown up, but I am not sure Marcus can survive without me.'

'You'll be fine, Alison, don't worry.' It seemed an inadequate response but it was all I could come up with at that moment.

The doctor came in. It wasn't the consultant we were expecting but one of their juniors, a male doctor who introduced himself as Dr Dunt. He seemed perfectly pleasant. He just wasn't the consultant.

He sat down and looked at her computer.

'So, Ms Daniels, you have had some bleeding?'

'Yes.'

'How many episodes?' he said, still looking at her computer.

'Three in total,' Alison said sheepishly.

'Hmmm, over how long?'

'About two weeks. It's stopped now.'

'That's good,' Dr Dunt said. 'Can I ask, do you bleed after intercourse?' He looked at Alison and then at me.

Wait a minute, I thought, *does this doctor think I am Alison's partner?* Surely not. Alison was a good twenty years older than me! But then I remembered that in medicine you are taught very early on not to make any assumptions. And I had to admit, sitting here with Alison in this private consultation, head to toe in Indian clothes, I looked very much like the ultimate 'internet order husband'. I imagined the doctor was wondering how much she had paid for me and where she had got me from.

I looked at Alison and could see she was thinking the same thing.

'Oh no, we've never seen any blood after intercourse,' Alison said, deliberately not giving anything away.

'And have you or your partner ever been treated for any sexually transmitted infections?' Dr Dunt asked, again looking at both of us.

'No, never,' Alison said.

'And your partner?' Dr Dunt asked again. He was looking directly at me.

There was a long pause. I bit my lip.

Alison interjected, 'Dr Dunt, this isn't my partner. This is my friend, Amir, he's come with me to the appointment. He is a doctor too, and I'm a nurse practitioner.' Alison was smirking. 'Sorry, we should have made that clear from the start.'

Dr Dunt breathed out loud, 'Oh okay, that makes more sense. I am sorry, I just didn't want to assume anything.'

'Don't worry,' Alison continued, 'I think you did wonderfully. If it were me I would want to know exactly what was going on, but you were very professional.'

I could see Dr Dunt was feeling uncomfortable. 'Er, thanks.'

'What would be the next investigation, Dr Dunt?' I asked.

'Yes, the next investigation, well, I would have to discuss it with my consultant but I imagine you will need a hysteroscopy to look into your womb and we could then take a biopsy.' He looked relieved to be talking about gynaecology again.

'Okay, that sounds like a reasonable next step,' Alison said. 'When will I get my appointment?'

'We will send it out in the post, but it's likely to be within the next two weeks,' Dr Dunt said.

We left shortly after.

'Hey Amir,' Alison said, 'that doctor thought we were a couple.'

'I know, and you let him carry on.'

Alison laughed. 'Well, you are an upgrade from Marcus; a girl can dream!'

Alison turned out to have a benign polyp which was removed easily and her symptoms settled down. We were all very relieved, nobody more so than Dr Dunt, who I think was just happy he would never have to see the pair of us again.

Alison and I have been firm friends for a decade now, from that very first time I encountered her with the nineteen-year-old 'wirgin'. Together we have dealt with more blood, pus and bodily fluids than is usual in most workplaces, I would imagine. We have also witnessed many intimate moments in our patients' lives, both heartbreaking and joyful, and all these shared experiences on a daily basis – with both Alison and my other colleagues – help to build a strong bond within the team. My colleagues and I are often on the phone to each other after a particularly long day in need of a debrief, and we support each other when we feel overwhelmed. The overriding sentiment was summarised recently by one of our newly qualified GPs, and I imagine is echoed throughout the NHS: 'I know it can be busy and I can find easier work elsewhere, but I stay for the team.'

Chapter Three

When you think about becoming a doctor, you have an image of the perfect GP in your mind, or at least I did. My mum never really took us to see the doctor when I was a child. Everything could be cured by a glass of hot milk mixed with turmeric and ginger. It tasted foul, but it seemed to work. She used it for colds, sore tummies, and even if we had fallen over and grazed ourselves outside. We were only ever taken to see the GP if we were very, *very* unwell. Every time we went we saw the same GP, Dr Fiona George.

Dr George was the perfect embodiment of what a GP should be.

I remember sitting in the waiting area under the watchful eye of the receptionists. It was very quiet, not like the waiting room in our surgery which is always buzzing with activity. There was a toy abacus in the corner and an old *Meg and Mog* book that had its first two pages missing. We aren't allowed toys in the waiting room now; it is classed as an infection risk. Children just play on their parents' mobile phones instead, which are probably far more risky.

Dr George would come out and call us in. She always wore a matching trouser suit with a smart blouse underneath. My mum would drag us away from the abacus and we would follow Dr George into her consulting room.

Chapter 3

It seemed to me that Dr George and my mum were more like friends than a doctor and patient. She would always greet my mum by her first name and ask about each of my sisters. My mum would take her in a homemade treat and in between their conversations about the family they might discuss whatever it was my mum had brought me in for. Dr George would then speak to me directly. She wasn't like the other adults I had encountered; she seemed genuinely interested in what I had to say and how my new school was. She would then scribble something down on her green prescription pad, hand it to my mother and always get up and open the door for us afterwards.

Dr George even came to see my dad at home after he had his first heart attack. We children were ushered upstairs out of the way so she could check him properly and not be distracted. I was fascinated by her leather briefcase; it was so neatly organised. Each item carefully folded and placed in individual pockets. Even her pen looked expensive. She politely declined my mum's offer to stay for lunch, saying she had other patients waiting to be seen.

My mum was devastated when Dr George retired.

'She has looked after this family for twenty-two years,' she said as she got ready to go the retirement party that was being held for Dr George's patients at the surgery. 'She gave you your first immunisations when you were a baby.' I watched my mum as she put her earrings on. She was wearing a shalwaar kameez that she usually reserved for weddings. I knew this meant it was a very important event.

As far as my mum is concerned, no other GP has ever lived up to Dr George.

When I applied to general practice, I wanted to be exactly like Dr George. I had a plan that I would know every one of my patients individually, know their families, ask about them each time they came in, and look at their holiday photographs on their phone. But I soon realised that Dr George practised in a very different time. As surgeries got larger, workload increased and GPs took on different roles. It became harder and harder for me to keep track of all of my patients.

If I wanted to keep up with modern-day general practice, I had to compromise. I was never going to be Dr George, but as well as doing my best for all the patients who came to see me, I could pull out those most vulnerable or the sickest and make sure I followed them through their illnesses.

Emily Ashworth was one such patient.

Emily was three years old when I first met her. Her mum, Wendy, had brought her in as she was feeling short of breath.

'Her lips were turning blue this morning,' Wendy said. 'And that was just from getting dressed.' I looked at Emily, whose gaze was flitting between her mum and something that had caught her eye on the table. She reached out, grabbed my otoscope and put the end that usually went down patients' ears into her mouth.

Her mum and I both went to take it off at her at the same time. I got there first.

'That's for people's ears, not mouths,' I said gently but firmly, placing it on the far side of the table, out of reach. She gave me a look and then put her thumb in her mouth instead.

'She said her chest hurt too,' Wendy continued. 'While she was eating breakfast, she said her chest was hurting and she looked short of breath. I don't know if it's just another infection or whether it is related to her heart condition.'

Emily had been diagnosed with heart problems on an ultrasound scan before she was born. It showed she had transposition of the great vessels, a rare but very serious condition where the main blood vessels leaving the heart are wired the opposite way round. This changes the way blood circulates through the body, meaning blood leaving the heart to the organs is low in oxygen. When she was born, it was found Emily also had a number of other congenital conditions of the heart, including pulmonary valve stenosis, where the valve controlling blood flow from the heart to the lungs is stiff and not opening properly. This means her blood is even lower in oxygen and she has a small hole in the middle of her heart.

All of this meant Emily had spent considerable time in hospital in her young life. Because a lot of the treatment she needed was so specialised she often had to travel to distant specialist centres to see the right doctor. She had had two major surgical procedures already to correct the direction of the flow of blood in her body, both of which were short-term fixes. The long-term plan was trickier; the shunt that had been inserted to correct the flow of the blood was only temporary and she would need definitive surgery in the future.

It was a complicated history, and often it can be a little intimidating seeing such complex patients in primary care, but these patients are just as prone to the ailments we see every day as everyone else, so it's important to still think horses rather than zebras when we hear the sound of hooves.

'Let's check her over, shall we?' I said.

Emily was so used to seeing doctors and being examined she was the most compliant three-year-old I had ever come across. Her temperature was a bit high, but nothing worrying. She lifted up her shirt so I could listen to her chest. It was the first time I had heard Emily's heart through my stethoscope, and there was a loud murmur that ran throughout it. Given her history, that was normal for her. Her chest sounded clear enough. I usually look in children's mouths at the end of the examination, as invariably they hate having their tongues pressed down with a wooden stick in order for me to get a good look at their throat. Emily was the opposite; she opened her mouth and stuck her tongue out the minute I picked up the dreaded tongue depressor.

'She's used to all of this,' her mum said.

Emily's tonsils were enlarged, with some pus on them. 'I think we have found the cause,' I said. 'Tonsillitis.' I sat back in my chair.

'So it isn't anything to do with her heart?' Wendy asked.

'I don't think so,' I said, shaking my head. 'Does she normally get a bit blue when she has an infection?' I asked. Wendy nodded. 'Usually, when we have an infection, especially with a temperature, the heart has to work a bit harder and faster. Emily's heart is already under some strain so working harder for it might mean she gets a bit blue around her mouth and nose.'

'Yes, the specialists at the hospital had said something similar,' Wendy replied.

'I think she probably needs some antibiotics to clear it up,' I said, typing up the prescription. Wendy didn't say anything. 'Does that sound okay to you, Mrs Ashworth?' She looked down at the floor and gave the faintest of nods.

'It's Miss Ashworth, I'm not married,' she said. 'Well, not any more.'

'Oh I'm sorry, that's my fault for assuming,' I said, feeling like an idiot.

'No, it's okay. She was still looking down at the floor but then suddenly looked up, as if out of a trance. 'We are fine, aren't we, Emily?' she said, cheerily. Emily ignored the question.

'Is it just the two of you at home?' I asked.

Chapter 3

'Oh no, Emily has two older sisters,' she said, still in her cheery voice. 'It's the four of us.'

I looked at Emily who was sitting on the chair next to her mum. Her little legs were too short to touch the floor so she waved them back and forth.

'It must be hard,' I said, 'taking Emily to all of her appointments and managing your other two daughters as well.'

'We survive, we support each other,' she said unconvincingly.

'Have you got much in the way of a support network?' I asked.

'Yes, my dad is close by and I have friends,' Wendy replied.

'You know, Miss Ashworth, being a carer for someone can be hard. It can be difficult to take time out for yourself,' I said. It is true; carers often get no respite and are constantly on the go.

Wendy stared straight ahead and was about to say something, but Emily spoke first.

'Mummy, can we go home now?'

Wendy looked at her daughter and nodded. I gave them their prescription for antibiotics and stood to open the door for them. I decided at that moment that I needed to familiarise myself with Emily's full medical history. Her notes contained lots of detailed letters from the hospital, and I made a mental note to take some time and go through them all. This was going to be one of those families I kept an eye on, just like Dr George.

I called in my next patient, a 57-year-old man named Percy Manford. If there was ever a stereotypical image of what a man from Yorkshire should look like, Percy Manford was it.

He wore a thick green woollen jacket that he unbuttoned to reveal a well-worn brown jumper over a white shirt. His green houndstooth trousers were a little too short for him and his boots were a little too big, as if to compensate. To finish the look, he wore a grey flat cap which he took off and placed on the chair next to him.

'Hi, Mr Manford, my name is Dr Khan. How can I help?'

'It is a bit of a strange one, doc,' he said in a broad Yorkshire accent. His cheeks were still red from the cold. 'I'm hoping you might be able to help.'

'Try me,' I said, leaning in.

'It's my sleep. I am just not sleeping very well,' he said. 'I always wake up at the same time every night at about two in the morning, then I just lie there and can't get back to sleep.'

There was nothing strange about insomnia, a lot of my patients come in with it. Sleep is precious, and without it we simply stop functioning. Often there is some type of underlying stress or anxiety that keeps sufferers awake and I offer them non-medical suggestions in the form of 'sleep hygiene', a series of things to do to help them get a better night's sleep.

'What do you think is keeping you awake at night?' I asked.

'Oh, I know exactly what is keeping me up at night,' Mr Manford said. 'It's the dreams I am having.'

'Dreams?' I asked. 'How so?'

'I keep having erotic dreams about my wife and then I can't get back to sleep,' Mr Manford said, sitting back in his chair.

'I'm sorry, Mr Manford, about your wife?' I was convinced I was missing a piece of this story.

'Oh, she is right there, lying next to me, fast asleep. But in my dreams we are making love.'

'Right.' I wasn't sure where the medical problem was here. 'And you don't make love in real life?'

'Nope, not since she went through the change. There's not been no lovemaking for over two years.'

Chapter 3

Percy Manford seemed to have a skill of being very direct and yet cryptic with his words all at the same time.

'Have you spoken with her about it?' I asked.

'You're joking, aren't you?' he snorted. 'She's made her feelings about the matter very clear in the past.'

'Well, I'm not sure there is much I can give you for vivid dreams, Mr Manford,' I said, a bit lost.

'Oh, I don't want anything for my dreams, I quite like them. It's the closest to lovemaking I'll get. I want you to give *her* something to help kick-start her libido,' he said, matter-of-factly.

'Oh I see,' I said, the penny finally dropping. 'Well, she would have to come in and see me herself, provided she actually thinks she needs something for her libido.'

'Can't you give me something to slip into one of her drinks or something?' he said, smiling.

'I'm afraid it doesn't work like that, Mr Manford. But I would be happy to discuss things with her.' This was turning out to be a strange consultation. 'Is there anything else I could help you with?'

'No, that was it,' he said, standing up and putting on his jacket.

'Well, thanks for coming in,' I said, opening the door for him.

As he left, I decided he was one those patients I could afford *not* to keep a close eye on.

Chapter Four

I work in an inner-city practice. Anyone who has worked in an inner-city environment will know what kind of opportunities and challenges that brings. As well as having a diverse set of staff, we serve a diverse population group, many of whom are migrants and have just arrived in the city with a list of medical problems that need sorting out. We pride ourselves on the service we provide patients who may not speak English. We have a Slovakian interpreter who will help translate our consultations for those patients from Eastern Europe and we have many South Asian doctors who can speak a multitude of languages for our South Asian patients, particularly the elderly ones.

It is often argued that they should learn to speak English, but to be honest that is not part of my job. My job is to find out why they have to come to see me and make them better.

Although English is my first language, I am also fluent in Urdu, Hindi and Punjabi, making me very popular with our patients from the Indian subcontinent. It is not uncommon for me to be presented with a medical file in a completely different language and the expectation is for me to be able to translate it within the allocated ten minutes. I was once at a GP conference in North Yorkshire and told a GP who worked in a lovely village in the North Yorkshire Dales that I could spend a whole day talking to patients and not speak a word of English.

Chapter 4

'Really, not a word of English?' he had said to me.

'Yep, I mean I would *prefer* to converse in English but if it's easier for my patients that we converse in their language and it puts them at ease then I am happy to do that. Do you have many non-English-speaking patients?' I asked him.

'None,' he replied, looking at me like I was some sort of strange specimen in a museum.

If I am being honest, I am overselling myself by claiming I am fluent in four languages. My linguistic skills have improved significantly since I started working at my practice. Prior to that, I was working in a surgery where I only ever spoke English. The thing is, when I was growing up I was spoken to in Urdu by my parents but I always replied to them in English. My sisters did the same. Actually I could speak everyday Urdu well enough but not *medical* Urdu. That was a whole different ballgame. We never talked about gallbladders, the pancreas or the lungs when we were talking at home, so I still had plenty to learn.

As a GP you don't get any more time to see patients when there are language barriers. If you are lucky you may get a double appointment but they are a rare commodity in a system where the demand is so high. Most of the time, you have just the ten minutes to deal with the language barrier and complete the consultation. It is a challenge to say the least.

I first got a sense of how much my Urdu skills were lacking when I got this job. I was two days in and had already seen a few patients who only spoke Urdu, so we tried our best to get by. There was a lot of gesturing and pointing involved. I was under the impression that I was doing well – there were a couple of words I didn't understand but the patients seemed to be leaving pretty happy after each consult. However, there was a word that two of my patients had mentioned to me that I hadn't come across before. Both of them had said they had pain in a place they referred to as their *bazu*. They both seemed well enough and I gave them some pain relief and sent them on their way.

I rang my mum up on the way home after the second time the word got mentioned.

'Mum, what does the word *bazu* mean? A couple of patients have mentioned it to me,' I asked.

'It means their arm,' she replied.

Panic set in. Both of these patients had had pain in their left arm! There was always a concern with left arm pain coming from a patient's heart. I turned the car around, got straight on to the phone to both patients and booked them in for a full cardiac work-up. Thankfully, they were both fine, but after that day I sat down with my mother for a lesson in medical Urdu. It got a bit awkward when we got to the reproductive system.

Today I was seeing a fourteen-year-old girl, Ivana, and her mum who only spoke Slovakian, so our interpreter had been called in. The girl had come in with pain in her leg that had been there for nearly a month. It wasn't affecting the way she was walking but the pain had stopped her from going to school a few times and was now keeping her awake at night.

As with most teenagers, Ivana herself seemed less concerned about the pain than her mum. But the mother did her best to explain the problem. I often find when using an interpreter for a consultation I end up somewhere between miming out what I'm saying as well as getting it translated, and often patients do the same. Although the interpreter was doing a perfectly good job, I was repeatedly pointing to my own leg with each question and closing my eyes and cradling my head when referring to sleep.

Chapter 4

I examined the young girl and couldn't find anything specific-ally abnormal. However, bone pain was an unusual symptom in children and language barriers can often lead to us missing the important nuances of a consultation, so I ordered some blood tests and sent Ivana for an x-ray of her leg. Ivana didn't seem bothered either way but Mum appeared to be appeased by the investigations. I promised to call them when I got the results.

I was typing up my consultation when Alison burst into my room.

'Amir, I think you need to come to room twelve, now.'

When Alison said 'now', I knew not to ask any questions. I grabbed my stethoscope and followed her to room twelve.

There was a female patient in her mid-fifties on the floor, and a medical student doing chest compressions on her.

'What happened?' I asked, kneeling by the patient.

'She was complaining of having a cough for the last two weeks,' the medical student said between compressions. 'She said her chest hurt when she coughed so I asked her to take a couple of sprays of her GTN spray to see if that would relieve the chest pain and she keeled over after doing so.'

GTN stands for 'glyceryl trinitrate'. It is a small pump device that people with angina carry around with them for when they get chest pain. It works by opening up the blood vessel to the heart, supplying it with more oxygen and thus relieving the pain. The problem is it can also drop your blood pressure and cause you to faint. It should not, however, cause you to have a cardiac arrest.

'Did you check to see if she had a pulse?' I asked the student.

'Yes, I couldn't find one,' she replied, still in full thrust.

I looked at the patient and caught a slight movement on her face. Had I just imagined that? No, definitely not. She seemed to be wincing with each compression. She was clearly not dead, as the medical student had thought, but had probably just passed out.

'Shall we stop the compressions for just a moment?' I said to the student.

'You're not supposed to stop compressions halfway through,' the student replied, carrying on pressing on the woman's chest.

'Stop the compressions NOW!' I said forcibly. The student was taken aback and stopped. There was a groan from the patient as she started to come round. She grimaced, feeling her chest.

'I think I will leave you to it,' Alison said, giving me a knowing look before leaving.

'What's her name?' I asked the student.

'Christine Melling,' the student replied quietly. She was starting to look a bit sheepish.

'Mrs Melling, my name is Dr Khan. It appears you passed out after taking your GTN spray. Joanne, our student, was worried about your pulse and felt chest compressions were the best thing to do. You may have a dull ache in the centre of your chest.'

'Dull ache!' Mrs Melling replied, sitting up. 'It feels like I've had all my ribs broken.' At least I *think* that's what she said. I was finding her very difficult to understand – her words were very unclear. *Not another comprehension problem*, I thought. Her name sounded English enough so I didn't think it was a language issue, but I was having difficulty making out a word of what she was saying and she had to keep repeating herself before I understood her. We were back to sign language again for the second time that day.

Chapter 4

The mystery was solved when Mrs Melling suddenly put her hand to her mouth and mumbled something, looking panicked. I couldn't understand her at all and was forced to ask her to repeat herself again. Eventually I got there.

'Did you say you've lost your false teeth?' I asked.

She nodded frantically.

'Joanne, did you see them?' I asked.

'Um, yes, I think they shot out when I started doing compressions.' Poor Joanne was clearly embarrassed.

We looked around the room. They must have been some pretty serious compressions to dislodge a set of false teeth, I thought. There were nowhere to be seen. Mrs Melling was starting to get agitated. Clearly these teeth were very important to her.

'Perhaps we could finish the consultation and then see if we can find your teeth?' I suggested. I wasn't hopeful. The consulting room wasn't big and there were only so many places the teeth could have been and we had checked them all.

Mrs Melling shook her head firmly. She clearly wasn't happy about that plan.

There was a knock on the door and Alison popped her head round.

'Just checking everything is okay?' she asked.

'Yes, we just can't seem to find Mrs Melling's teeth. They came out during the chest compressions,' I said.

'Oh yes, I picked them up and put them in her pocket for safekeeping. I know how important dentures are, my dad is always losing his!' Alison said casually before leaving again.

Mrs Melling felt in her pocket. She mumbled something unintelligible then produced a pair of dentures and popped them back into her mouth. 'That's better,' she said, perfectly clearly.

I ushered Mrs Melling into my room so I could finish seeing her for her cough and now her broken ribs. She understood what had happened and why, and agreed it was an easy mistake to make. The medical student apologised profusely. I felt sorry for Joanne and offered to give her a tutorial on how to check if someone was alive or dead. Hopefully it wouldn't take too much time.

Every now and again in general practice you will get a set of results back that makes you just stop for a moment and let out an audible gasp. Three days after seeing her, Ivana's blood results arrived. They were grossly abnormal: her white cell count was sky high and her red blood cell count was low. There was also a note from the pathologist at the bottom of them: '*Blast cells seen urgent clinical review needed.*'

Blast cells are immature white blood cells, and there really shouldn't be many (if any) circulating around your blood. It would suggest the bone marrow is churning them out at a rate that the body cannot keep up with. They fill up the space in the bone marrow so it can do very little else, including make your red blood cells.

Ivana's blood results suggested she had a malignancy, most likely leukaemia.

When these kinds of results come back to doctors, we usually have a mix of emotions. Firstly, there is empathy for the patient and the fact they are likely to have a serious medical problem. Secondly, there is huge relief that you did the tests in the first place and picked it up. Nobody wants to be the doctor who missed cancer in a patient, though with the sheer numbers of patients a GP sees, the likelihood is that this will happen at least once in our careers.

Chapter 4

It was now vitally important that I contacted Ivana and her family *today* and got them admitted to hospital for an urgent review. The issue was they didn't speak English so I would need them to come in with an interpreter, and in any case I really didn't want to tell them over the phone. This was definitely a face-to-face type of conversation.

I dialled the number that was on Ivana's notes. No answer. I tried again. No answer. I brought up her mum's records and dialled the number on there. An elderly sounding woman answered the phone, but she couldn't speak English either. The conversation went round and round in circles with me trying to find out where Mum was, but eventually she got cross and hung up.

I was stuck. I still had three more patients to see before the end of my morning clinic so I asked one of the receptionists to keep trying Ivana while I saw them. At the end of my clinic, I went to see if she had had any success.

'Sorry, Amir, it just keeps ringing and ringing. I tried several household contacts too but either nobody answers or they can't understand what I am saying,' she told me.

I went back to my room. I was going to have to go to Ivana's home and just hope she would be in.

I asked the Slovakian interpreter, Peter, to come with me. His shift had finished ten minutes earlier and he was due to go home, but he kindly agreed (I promised I would buy him a drink at the Christmas party, which was four months away).

Ivana didn't live too far away so we decided to walk. The house was a small back-to-back terrace with a uPVC front door with two frosted glass panels running down each side of it. We knocked hard. No answer. We tried several more times to no avail. Just as we were about to give up, we saw movement behind the frosted glass. A man in his twenties opened the door.

'Hi, it's Dr Khan from the surgery. I am looking for Ivana; does she live here?' I asked. He looked confused. I looked at Peter who translated it for me. The man shook his head and said something.

'He says Ivana no longer lives here,' Peter told me. 'He isn't sure where she is.'

This was strange. I had only seen her three days ago; she couldn't have gone far. 'Can you ask him if there is anyone else at home who might know where she is?' Peter translated the request. The man shook his head, I didn't need that translating. We thanked him and left.

I dropped Peter off at the bus station and wondered what I was going to do. In most cases I would have thought I had done enough in trying to track down the patient, but this wasn't most cases. This was a child with a potential leukaemia. Knowing we didn't have the correct address for her meant we couldn't write to her asking her to see us urgently. I had a brainwave; perhaps she had been admitted to hospital? I rang the hospital but there was no record of her being brought there either.

I went back to the surgery as my afternoon clinic was about to start. I saw my patients but my mind kept harking back to Ivana. I kept having visions of her lying dead somewhere because I hadn't managed to get her to the hospital in time. The reception staff continued to phone both Ivana and her mum but got no response.

That night, I switched my computer on when I was back at home and brought up Ivana's records. I checked to see if she had been for the x-ray I had ordered but it didn't look as if she had. I picked up my mobile phone and dialled her number again. It rang out. She had literally disappeared.

Chapter 4

It isn't unusual for our Eastern European patients to change addresses without telling us. They can come to the country and initially stay with relatives and friends and use that address to register at the practice. They then move to another home when it becomes available for them. There is a thriving Slovakian community in the area and I have often found more than one family living at one address. It wasn't usually a problem, until now.

I arrived at work the next day tired, as I hadn't slept well. I went straight to the kitchen to make a coffee and was greeted by Henry, our manager.

'Amir, you don't look well,' he said, taking one look at me.

'Don't, Henry, I haven't slept all night.' I told him about what had happened.

'How old is she?' Henry asked.

'Fourteen.'

'Well, why don't you just ring up her school and see if she's there today?' Henry said casually as he tossed his teabag into the bin.

I stared at him. 'Henry, you're a genius!' I said, going in for a high five.

'Watch the tea!' Henry said.

As soon as 9 a.m. came, I rang Ivana's school to see if she was there. She was. A wave of relief washed over me. I told the receptionist I needed to speak urgently with her and that I would wait until she came out of class. Ideally, I would have spoken with her mum but I had no way to contact her.

Ivana's English wasn't good but I managed to make her understand she needed to come and see me and she gave me her mum's new mobile phone number. She also agreed to come in.

I purposefully booked them the last appointment of the morning; that way if I ran over there would be nobody waiting. I asked Peter the interpreter to join us.

Ivana was still wearing her school uniform when she arrived, a grey skirt and white shirt. She had deliberately tied her tie to make it look very short, something a lot of the teenagers were doing. Her mum, Irene, was in her work uniform, a light blue tunic with the name of her employer sewn onto the pocket. They both sat down. This time Ivana did look worried.

'Thank you for coming to see me at such short notice,' I said. 'Ivana, how are you feeling?'

Peter translated for me, Ivana looked at me and then at him before saying something in Slovakian.

'She says she is still tired but okay,' Peter said.

'Did you manage to go for the x-ray?' I asked. She shook her head and muttered something.

'Not yet, she has not had time,' Peter said. Irene asked a question. 'Mum wants to know if you have the blood test results?'

'Yes, I have them,' I said.

Breaking this kind of news is always difficult and has to be done carefully. It's hard enough when both parties speak the same language. Having a triangulated consultation made it very difficult, but there was no other way.

'When you came in to see me last time, tell me what you were worried about,' I asked. I was trying to find out where they were in their thought process, as it would give me a better idea of how to approach this.

'She says she was worried that Ivana might have low iron levels, that's why she was so tired all the time,' Peter said, translating Irene's words.

I nodded. 'Well, the results have shown something, but it's not as simple as an iron deficiency,' I said. A warning shot.

As Peter translated, there was a palpable change to the mood in the room.

'What have they shown?' Peter said on behalf of Ivana and Irene.

I took a deep breath. 'Ivana, the bloods suggest there may be something wrong with your bone marrow. Your white cells are very high and your red cells are very low,' I paused, waiting for Peter to translate that part for me.

Neither of them said anything as they continued to look at me.

'When we get results like this, we have to worry about a type of blood cancer,' I said, looking at Ivana.

The word cancer didn't need translating. Irene drew a breath in and put a hand to her chest. 'Cancer?' she said. Peter translated my words in full. Ivana's eyes widened and she bit on her lower lip. I had to carry on.

'I wouldn't be doing my job properly if I wasn't honest with you,' I said. 'I am very worried about the results.'

'What kind of cancer?' Irene asked via Peter.

'There is a worry this may be leukaemia,' I said flatly.

I let the word hang for a moment.

'Is it bad?' Ivana said in English. It broke my heart.

'Ivana, I am hoping we have caught this early. If this is leukaemia, then the treatment options are good but the specialists will be able to explain this better than me,' I said.

I had worked in a children's hospital during my junior doctor days, spending four months on the oncology ward. I had a very small part, collecting blood samples and writing up notes, but I had an idea what lay in store for Ivana. The outlook for childhood leukaemia is good, but the treatment is aggressive. In my experience, the intensity of the treatment changed the children and families forever. Ivana faced long periods in hospital; she would have to travel to another city for a lot of her appointments and Irene would likely need a lot of time off work.

'What happens now?' Irene asked, her eyes brimming with tears. I passed her a tissue.

'I will speak to the paediatric team at the hospital, I think they will want to see Ivana today.'

Irene nodded. Ivana didn't say anything.

'Do you mind me asking where Ivana's father is?' I asked. It might be best if I spoke to him directly too. Irene said something to Peter.

'He died three years ago in Slovakia. A work accident,' Peter said. Poor Peter, I hadn't told him what the bloods had shown beforehand so this was news to him. I imagined this would have had an emotional impact on him too and it is unlikely he would have had all the communication skills training I had been given.

'I am sorry to hear that,' I said. 'I know this is a lot of information to take in, but do you have any questions you want to ask me?'

Ivana said something to Peter.

'Do they have to go to hospital now, or can they go home first?' Peter said.

'You can go home to pack a bag,' I said. 'It is likely they will keep you or send you to see the specialists at the bigger hospital, so best be prepared for that.'

They nodded. Irene said she would have to call the school and her work to let them know what was going on. I spoke with the paediatric team at the hospital who agreed to see Ivana that day. I printed off a letter and gave it to Irene.

'I know things will be very difficult,' I said to both of them, handing over the letter. 'But if you need anything at all, please let me know.'

Chapter 4

Irene took the letter and thanked me. I asked Peter to accompany them both to reception and update their address and phone numbers on our records. Something told me I would need to know both of these in the future.

After they left, I started typing up my notes. I thought about how it would feel being in a foreign country, not speaking the language, and getting a diagnosis like this. The hospitals would be geared up to put support in place for them, but I couldn't help but think it would only make the fear and worry worse.

I spoke to Alison afterwards about the case.

'Aren't you glad you did those blood tests, Amir?' she said.

'It was just luck, Alison. Normally I wouldn't do blood tests on a kid. It was just dumb luck,' I said.

Ivana was diagnosed with acute lymphoblastic leukaemia. I didn't see much of her during her treatment, as the hospital did most things for her. I wrote a letter on Irene's request to her workplace, explaining to them that she would need extended periods off to take her daughter to and from the hospital for treatment.

We had caught the disease early enough for the treatment to be effective. After a year, Ivana was in remission, and she now goes for six-monthly checks at the hospital. Her education suffered as a result, but she was allowed to re-sit her school year. Sadly, Irene's workplace was not as understanding and her employment was terminated due to the time off she needed. She struggled financially as a result, but when she last came to see me she told me she had an interview at a local supermarket. I promised I would keep everything crossed for her.

Chapter Five

I have heard the phrase 'don't work with children or animals' mentioned when I listen to actors or TV people talk about their work. You see a lot of children in general practice, and you get used to the crying and the screaming during examinations, it's all par for the course. Actually, we *prefer* it when children cry and scream; it means they can't be that ill, as they still have lots of energy and fight in them. It's the quiet, listless children you have to worry about. We don't see many animals in our surgery, which I guess makes sense since we are GPs and not vets. But never say never.

It was the summer holidays, which were a strange time of year for us; the hot weather meant we saw less of the acute infectious stuff, but it meant those who had struggled against the masses to get an appointment with us for their ongoing chronic problems now found it easier to get one.

In the past people would say the summer months are the least busy. You're not allowed to say the word 'quiet' in the healthcare profession, as there is a certain superstition around it. By saying it you are inviting the hordes of sick people who would have otherwise stayed at home to darken your door. It's referred to as the 'Q' word and it must never be spoken in full – a bit like Voldemort.

Chapter 5

I had a medical student with me, whose name was Ibrahim. He wasn't just your average medical student; he was an international medical student from Kuwait. He was here on exchange to see how our healthcare system worked in the UK. I had been on my best behaviour all day; I was after all an ambassador for the UK, representing the NHS. I couldn't have him give a bad report of me to the Prince of Kuwait.

'Is it usually this quiet on a Friday?' he asked.

I couldn't believe it; he had said it. We were so nearly there. I couldn't help the scowl that appeared on my face – all NHS workers have perfected it for the minute anyone says the 'Q' word. I had to remind myself that it wasn't his fault that he didn't know the rules.

'Let's hope it stays that way,' I replied casually. Inside I was praying hard for nothing to scupper the last thirty minutes. *It's only an old superstition,* I told myself, *something the nurses tell all new doctors when we start, it's not true.*

As I was finishing my secret prayers, the phone rang. It was from reception.

'Hello?' I said, my voice a little more high pitched than I was planning.

'Hi Amir, it's Ivy – are you free?' Ivy was one of my favourite receptionists. I found her fascinating. Originally from South Africa, she now lived in a caravan on the outskirts of the city with her husband, Lloyd. My favourite thing about Ivy was that she wore a different wig to work almost every day and had the most perfectly manicured fingernails I had ever seen. She was very glamorous.

'Yes, just filing some blood results,' I said. I wasn't filing blood results, but I had to sound busy and couldn't very well say I was quizzing Ibrahim about his upcoming wedding, which sounded very extravagant.

'There is a lady here with her two-year-old daughter – she says the daughter has a new rash. Can you see her?'

'Yes of course, just put her name on the end of my list and I will call her in.' I actually didn't mind this in the slightest; rashes can be a sign of a serious infection in children and it would give me the opportunity to show Ibrahim how to examine a child with this presentation.

If this was all that resulted from saying the 'Q' word, then I thought I had got off pretty lightly.

I pressed the icon on my computer that called the patient and her mum in from the waiting area.

There was a knock on the door and a young-looking mum and two children entered the room. I hadn't met any of them before, as they were newly registered with us. One of the children, the poorly girl, was sitting in a very well-used pram. She had been eating Wotsits and her fingers were still orange from the crisp dust, as was her mouth. Some of the crisps had clearly fallen out of the bag and were nestled between the child and the seat of the pram. The older child, a boy, was playing on a hand-held games console. He managed to walk through the door and sit on the chair all without looking up once from his computer screen.

I immediately had an affinity towards the mum of these two children. She looked tired – it was a hot day in the middle of the summer. Sometimes, all you can do to keep your kids quiet is to give them a bag of crisps and a games console. I get it.

'Hi, my name is Dr Khan and this is Ibrahim, one of our students. How can I help?' I said, smiling at the mum and the girl.

'It's Tiffany, she's got these spots on her chest – they just came up this afternoon and they're itchy,' Mum replied in a broad Yorkshire accent.

'Okay, we will take a look, but before we do – has she had a temperature or been sick?' I asked.

'No, she's been fine – but it's hot so she might have a temperature, I'm not sure.'

'We will check. Is she drinking and passing urine okay?'

'Yes.'

'Has she done anything out of the ordinary today, or come into contact with something new?'

Mum paused for thought. 'She's been playing out all day on the grass, that's about it.'

'Okay, let's take a look. Do you mind if I talk to Ibrahim about what I am looking for when we examine children?'

'No, that's fine.'

Mum unstrapped Tiffany from the pram and placed her on the examination couch, stripping her down to her nappy.

I beckoned Ibrahim to come over with me and he stood behind me as I examined the child.

Teaching students is something I do every day in clinic. It's become second nature to me.

'So, when you are examining a rash on a child, Ibrahim, the first thing to do is to try to blanch it. If it doesn't blanch it might be meningococcal septicaemia, which is obviously very dangerous,' I said in my most knowledgeable voice. I already knew by looking at the rash it was nothing serious, but I liked a bit of drama when students were around.

As I was talking, a strange noise behind me caught my attention. Ibrahim was a mouth breather. Why hadn't I noticed that before? That was definitely the kind of thing I would pick up on immediately. I was a bit disappointed in myself.

In fact, Ibrahim was a really loud mouth breather; he was putting me off the job in hand.

'Dr Khan, I am allergic to cats,' Ibrahim whispered behind me.

What an odd time to bring such a thing up, I thought. I ignored it, and got on with the examination.

I continued to examine Tiffany, who was doing her best to wriggle off the couch.

'Honestly, Dr Khan, I am very allergic to cats,' Ibrahim said, louder this time between breaths, 'and I haven't got my EpiPen with me.'

'Okay, Ibrahim, I will bear that in mind, thank you. Now, when describing a rash, it's important to estimate the size of each lesion as this will tell you if——'

'Dr (gasp) Khan (breath), I (gasp) think (gasp) I (gasp) have (gasp) to (gasp) leave.' Ibrahim was panting now.

Okay, enough was enough – I turned around to see why Ibrahim was behaving so strangely, one hand keeping Tiffany from falling off the couch. As I turned, I saw that Ibrahim was as white as a sheet. He wasn't just a mouth breather; he was struggling to breathe.

Oh shit, he was going to collapse, I could tell, but I couldn't catch him without letting go of Tiffany.

I handed Tiffany back to Mum, and as I did so Ibrahim fell backwards, collapsing onto the floor. His flailing arms hit the pram on the way down, turning it sideways. At the same time, TWO CATS that had been sitting quietly on the bottom shelf of the pram shot out into my consulting room.

Tiffany started wailing. The boy continued to play on his console.

I went to check on Ibrahim – his breathing had gone quiet and his eyes were closing. He was having an anaphylactic

64

reaction, one of the most serious forms of allergic reaction. These can be fatal if not treated promptly.

I ran to my desk and pressed my panic alarm.

All clinical rooms have a panic alarm, which are designed to alert other staff members to an emergency in your room. Normally within seconds they would descend like an arriving cavalry. The problem was, I was working at one of our branch sites and the only other person here was Ivy. She would have to do.

The door flew open and in she came.

'Is everything—' Ivy never finished that sentence. She didn't see Ibrahim lying on the floor and tripped over his now shutting-down body. She landed face first on the floor – her beautiful purple wig shooting off and disappearing into the corner of the room. 'Ivy, are you okay?' I shouted, my attention now being pulled in several different directions at once.

'Yes, I'm fine,' she gasped, clambering to her feet. She looked very different without her wig. 'What's happened to your student?'

'Anaphylaxis – we need the crash trolley; can you get it please? And call an ambulance!' The crash trolley is where all surgeries keep their emergency equipment and drugs. It's usually bright red and it's the first thing you show to new employees on their induction. It's where our adrenaline was kept, which is what Ibrahim needed – right now.

Ivy got up and rushed out of the room, this time carefully avoiding Ibrahim's prone body.

While she was gone I asked the mum and children to wait in reception.

'Mummy, what about our cats?' wailed Tiffany.

Dammit, I had forgotten about the escaped cats – where the hell had they gone? They were nowhere to be seen.

'Don't worry, we'll get the cats back to you soon,' I said, trying to sound as hopeful as I could.

Ivy returned with the crash trolley. I found the syringe with the adrenaline in and attached a needle to it.

'Right, Ibrahim, I am going to have to lower your trousers to inject this into your thigh,' I said.

Ibrahim whispered something that sounded like, 'Okay.'

In the adrenaline went, and I put an oxygen mask on him. I monitored his pulse and oxygen levels, which seemed to be holding. My own heart rate started to come down as I saw Ibrahim's condition improve.

Real-life collapses are actually very scary, even as an experienced GP. How I wished I could go back to the days where I found students doing chest compressions on live patients and the most stressful thing was finding their false teeth afterwards.

Soon there was another knock on the door and two paramedics came in with huge bags of equipment. Ibrahim was attached to a more sophisticated monitor and a new oxygen cylinder. He was well enough to get into their chair and be wheeled off to the hospital.

I tried to say something cheery as he left to lift the mood. 'Well, that will teach you to say the "Q" word,' I laughed.

It didn't work. The paramedics just looked at me blankly and I realised that Ibrahim would have no idea what I was talking about.

'Okay, get well soon!' I said, ushering them out of the door.

I shut the door and closed my eyes. I know I said I liked drama when students were around but this is not what I meant. As I slumped against my desk, I heard a noise. I opened my eyes.

The cats. Who on earth brings cats out without putting them in a cat carrier? I mean, they're cats! I had to find them.

Chapter 5

The noise had come from under the couch. I got down on my hands and knees and started making that kissing noise that I had heard people do when they wanted to attract the attention of a cat.

'Come on, kitty,' I said in a child-like voice. What the hell was I doing? I was a GP in a GP's surgery, crawling around on all fours, looking for two escaped cats. This is not what I had signed up for.

I manoeuvred my head so I could see under the couch. I could make out the silhouette of one of them. I reached out to grab it, hoping it wouldn't scratch. It felt soft in my hand and wasn't putting up a fight. *Thank God for small miracles*, I thought.

I pulled it out. It wasn't the cat. It was Ivy's wig.

Ivy and I spent thirty minutes looking for the cats, both of which had managed to run out of the room during the commotion. We returned them safely to their owners and I explained that Tiffany's rash looked like insect bites from playing outside, so she wouldn't need any further treatment.

Mum promised to buy a cat carrier for future trips and thankfully Ibrahim made a full recovery.

Ivy and I had a debrief afterwards over a cup of tea and some custard creams. Her real hair was grey – I hadn't expected that – and it was tied in the tiniest plait I had ever seen. I rather liked it. The conversation mainly revolved around how nice her actual hair was and how she shouldn't always wear wigs. Neither of us mentioned the 'Q' word.

Of course, not all animals we encounter are of the live variety. Sometimes the stuffed toy versions are just as important.

My final patient that day was Emily Ashworth, the young girl with the heart condition. It had been nearly two years since our

67

first encounter and Emily was now five years old. I had seen the family a few times since. I felt I was building up a good relationship with them. I had already met the other daughters so was starting build up a picture in my mind about the dynamics of the family.

Wendy and Emily's dad were no longer together; she described the relationship as strained but felt the girls were coping well.

Emily was due to have the shunt in her heart replaced. She had outgrown the ones that had been put in when she was younger. Surgeons from London were coming up to Yorkshire to be part of the team that performed the procedure. Their plan was to open Emily up and take a look at her heart and decide what kind of shunt would be best for her. They would also use the opportunity of the inspection to plan Emily's definitive surgery once she was old enough. The idea of this huge operation performed by a team of surgeons from across the country was one of the times that made me stop and wonder at the NHS. For all of its limitations it was still an incredible organisation to be part of.

Wendy and Emily sat down. Emily had a stuffed giraffe with her.

'Who is this you have brought with you?' I asked, pointing at the giraffe. Emily knew me pretty well now and her initial shyness had long dissipated.

'My friend, Sophie,' she said, handing me the giraffe. It looked like Sophie had seen better days. 'Sophie is coming with me to the hospital,' she said.

'Oh wow, is Sophie going to be as brave as you?' I asked. Emily nodded, taking Sophie back. 'How are things?' I asked, turning to Wendy.

'They are good, everything is on track. Emily is having her operation at the end of this week. I just wanted you to check her over. The doctors at the hospital said to bring her in a few days before to make sure she doesn't have any signs of an infection.'

This was standard before a large operation, so I grabbed my stethoscope and examined Emily. Everything seemed fine. 'And how are you feeling about the surgery?' I asked Wendy.

She let out a sigh, pressed something on her phone and handed it to Emily. 'Emily, do you want to look at some cartoons while Mummy talks to Dr Khan?' Emily wasn't going to say no to that offer. She took the phone, dumped Sophie on the floor and started watching *Paw Patrol*.

'I am just so worried, Dr Khan,' Wendy began. 'The surgeons explained everything to me but I haven't been able to sleep all week. The consent form I had to sign said there was a risk of death with the procedure. Death. Do you think it's the right thing to do?'

Wendy looked at me expectantly. I glanced at Emily who was engrossed with her show.

'All I can say is that without the surgery, Emily's heart will get very poorly and the risks will be higher. I am not sure we have any other option,' I said.

Wendy and I were only a few months apart in age. I often thought this when she came in. We had grown up in the same city and gone to neighbouring schools. It could have easily been me sitting where she was now.

'It's just so hard to know what to do for the best. It feels like I have no control,' she said. 'Like whatever happens to Emily is not my decision.'

I empathised with that. Refusing the surgery meant almost certain death for Emily, but the surgery came with its own risks. I imagined that Wendy had seen so many specialists, her head was spinning.

'She has the best doctors in the country performing the surgery, we have to keep thinking about that,' I said gently.

Wendy nodded. She picked the stuffed giraffe off the floor and handed her to Emily, who hugged her close. 'Come on you,' she said to her daughter.

Emily looked up and flashed me a big grin. 'Sophie says goodbye!' she said, waving its leg at me.

'Goodbye to you too, Sophie,' I said, waving back. As I watched the little girl leave, holding her stuffed giraffe tightly against her chest, I reflected that whoever said you should never work with children and animals was missing out on something special.

Chapter Six

It had been a bad start to the day. I had had a complaint. *An actual written complaint from a patient.* It has been a long while since I had had a complaint; in fact, I prided myself on my lack of negative feedback. But sadly, my run had come to an end.

All doctors dread complaints. We were told during our training period we were all definitely going to get complaints, probably even sued, but we all secretly thought we would be the exception to the rule. Provided you did everything right, stuck to the guidelines and were nice, how could anyone possibly complain about you? We soon learned that was not how it worked.

I read the letter in dismay. The patient was not happy to have received an SMS message on the weekend informing her to make a non-urgent appointment to see the GP within two weeks. The truth is there just isn't enough time in the working week for me to do all the work that is required of me. By the time I have finished seeing all my patients, I have a mountain of hospital letters and blood results to work through. Staying at work late would mean no time spent with my family, so I compromise. I log on to the system from home and do my work from there. That way, I am technically at home with the family but at the same time catching up on work. In this case I had sent the patient an SMS from home over the weekend as I had not had time to do it during surgery hours on the Friday.

It had backfired that time. The patient stated she had been worried all weekend and, due to the surgery being closed, had nobody to allay her fears. I put the letter into my bag, I didn't have time to reply to it then. I would log on from home tonight and respond to her then. And yes, the irony of that wasn't lost on me.

Sometimes we get it wrong when a patient feels we have let them down. Other times we get it right when we get to know a patient really well and do everything we can for them. But this emotional involvement in a patient's life can take as much of a toll on you as a complaint.

Ishaq and Zara Sinha were well known to me. I had looked after Ishaq's dad when he had been diagnosed with an aggressive brain tumour. It had been a complex diagnosis. He had been away in India and his legs had suddenly stopped working. It wasn't a gradual decline in their function; it happened suddenly while he was in the bank. He told me he had just changed some British pounds to Indian rupees and was making his way to the car when he felt his legs go numb and heavy, and then all of a sudden he was unable to walk. He fell to the floor and some onlookers had to help him get to the hospital. An MRI scan showed he had a tumour in the base of his spine, but this turned out to be a secondary tumour. The primary was found later after a seizure he had while in the hospital, a brain tumour. Unfortunately for Mr Sinha, he had the most aggressive type of brain tumours, a glioblastoma. The doctors in India offered Mr Sinha surgery to help debulk the tumour, this was to reduce the size of it, but there was no cure. Mr Sinha decided to return home to the UK and spend his last few months with his family.

Mr Sinha only spoke Hindi, so, when it came to assigning him a lead clinician, it was felt that someone who could communicate with him easily would be best. Although Hindi and Urdu are classed as two distinct languages, they are almost identical. I know this because every Friday night my dad would rent the latest Bollywood movie from the Asian video store and we would sit down and watch them. And this probably where I learned most of my Urdu/Hindi from – and also the fact that whenever it rains you *must* go out and dance.

Knowing the languages were very similar was something I had largely kept secret. I'd listed both on my CV in the 'fluent languages' section so that when I applied for a job they would think I could speak more languages than I actually could and looked clever. It's a bit like saying I can speak both English and Scottish. Although, at the time of being appointed to Mr Sinha, my mum had fully schooled me in medical Urdu and I had extensive practice in speaking the language working in an inner city environment. I was now actually fluent, and not just the pretend kind of fluency that I had referred to on my CV.

When I first met Mr Sinha he was lying in a hospital bed the district nurses had ordered for him and placed in his living room. It faced the television and he was watching cricket. I had asked him if, before the incident with his leg, he had had any warning symptoms of his glioblastoma.

'I had some nausea,' Mr Sinha said, 'but I didn't think anything of it. I just thought I was in India; everyone gets a bit sick.'

'No headaches or problems with your vision?' I asked.

'No,' he said, looking at the television which was now muted, 'but my wife said I had been nicer to her the last few months.'

I smiled. 'Well they do say personality change is a symptom.'

We both laughed.

Mr Sinha was a huge cricket fan, when it wasn't being played live he would watch old matches and still get excited about them.

Whenever I went to see him to manage his pain medication we would always talk about the cricket. To be honest, I know nothing about cricket, but he enjoyed telling me about what had been going on that day and I was happy to listen. Very little of what we talked about was actual medicine; as well as cricket we talked about politics, the weather and his grandchildren. Most of all we talked about how he felt about dying. He wasn't scared, that's what stuck with me. One day he asked me a funny question: 'Amir, are you afraid of death?'

As a GP we see death all the time, but we never really stop and reflect on our own mortality. 'To be honest, I think I am,' I answered. I didn't see the point in lying to him.

'Don't be,' he said. He didn't elaborate further. I wanted him to tell me he knew something I didn't, that I needn't be scared, that none of us should be. He didn't, he just left that thought hanging in the air.

He died the next day. I attended his funeral. It isn't something I am able to do very often for my patients, but I had spent a lot of time with Mr Sinha and his family and it felt like the right thing to do.

Mr Sinha's son, Ishaq, had found the loss of his father difficult to come to terms with. Mr Sinha had run an accountancy firm in the city, which Ishaq was now taking the lead on, something he was struggling to do alongside his grief. He came to see me at the surgery to talk about how best to cope with bereavement, occasionally he was accompanied by his wife, Zara.

A few months after Mr Sinha had died, they came in together. I was expecting another supportive conversation about how Ishaq was coping after his father's death but sensed an altogether different vibe when they both walked in.

'Is everything okay?' I asked, putting down my pen.

Chapter 6

'I'm pregnant!' Zara blurted out excitedly.

'Oh wow, that's great news!' I replied, smiling.

'Yes, Ishaq's Mum is over the moon – she has already started knitting little cardigans and booties for the baby.' Zara couldn't contain her excitement. 'I think having a baby around will really help her, she has been missing his dad so much.'

'We were hoping you could confirm the pregnancy here too,' Ishaq said.

Confirming pregnancies wasn't something we liked to do in surgery. The pregnancy tests from the shops were just as accurate as ours, and there was rarely any difference in the result. But I didn't want to dampen their spirits so agreed.

Zara had come prepared. She produced a pot of urine from her handbag and excitedly handed it over to me. I dipped it using one of our pregnancy tests and waited.

Usually doing a pregnancy test at a GP surgery is a tense moment. Anyone who comes to the GP and needs us to do a test hasn't generally thought about the possibility of their tummy pain or bleeding being due to pregnancy, and as a rule they don't want to be pregnant. We then go on to have a very different discussion about the future of the pregnancy.

The test takes about one minute to give a result. Very occasionally, ours give a different answer to the shop-bought ones. I was hoping this wouldn't be one of those times.

It wasn't; it was positive. There were lots of hugs and talking about the dos and don'ts of being pregnant and then they left. It was a good moment, some good news. We don't often get to give good news to patients, so I relished the experience.

As the sad news of Mr Sinha's death turned to the good news of Zara's pregnancy I saw less and less of the two of them. The pregnancy, like most pregnancies, was managed by the expert midwives at the local hospital. Zara went over her due date but eventually gave birth to a baby girl they named Maaha.

It is an Indian tradition to give out sweets to close family and friends when a baby is born. When Maaha was born, Ishaq bought a mountain of sweets and chocolates to the practice. They kept us going for days, which is a miracle in itself as usually boxes of chocolates are devoured within seconds of them being opened at our surgery.

When she was brought in for her first set of immunisations with our practice nurse I made a point of going out into the waiting room for a cuddle and catch up with the family.

'How is she doing?' I asked.

'She is wonderful,' Zara beamed. 'Tiring, but wonderful.'

'I bet she is,' I said looking at Maaha. She was curled up in her car seat, wrapped in a blanket and wearing a hat that her grandmother must have knitted for her. Her tiny hands were hidden inside a pair of mitts.

'She won't be looking so relaxed after her injections,' Ishaq said, adjusting Maaha's hat which was now slipping over her eyes.

'Stop it, I am already nervous,' Zara said, jabbing him with her elbow.

Two months would pass before I saw Maaha again; it was while I was on call. Zara had phoned up to say Maaha wasn't feeding very well and had developed a temperature, so I asked her to bring her straight down.

Ishaq was still at work, so Zara came alone.

'She has been off all day, not interesting in taking her milk and just not herself,' Zara said, as Maaha lay on her lap. There was no car seat this time, it had been left in the car.

I nodded. 'And you mentioned a temperature?'

Chapter 6

'Yes, she felt warm, that's why I rang,' Zara said, the panic rising in her voice.

'Have you noticed any new rashes on her?'

Zara shook her head. 'No.'

'When was the last time she passed urine?' I asked, not taking my eyes of Maaha.

'She had a wet nappy last night, but she hasn't had much to drink so she hasn't done anything today.'

Zara felt the front of Maaha's nappy for confirmation, and shook her head again.

'Okay, let's examine her,' I said, gesturing for Zara to place Maaha on the examination couch.

I unbuttoned her Babygro and removed the vest she had on underneath. I observed Maaha's body as she lay there in just her nappy. Her breathing was shallow and rapid. Every time she exhaled she let out a little grunt of effort. I placed my stethoscope on her chest to listen to her heart. Normally the shock of the cold surface of the stethoscope on their skin makes most children jolt, but Maaha barely moved. Her heart rate was going so fast it was difficult to keep count. I looked at her feet; they were beginning to mottle.

At four months old, Maaha clearly had some kind of infection that was causing the small blood vessels in her feet and legs to constrict and shut down. On top of this she was dangerously dehydrated.

'Zara, Maaha has a serious infection. I am going to call for an ambulance,' I said as calmly as possible. 'I am also going to ask for some help from my colleagues while the ambulance comes.'

Zara didn't say anything.

I put out a call for help. Aiden one of my GP colleagues rushed in, followed by Tonia a receptionist.

'A child with sepsis. Tonia we need a blue-light ambulance. Aiden, would you mind getting the crash trolley.' They both disappeared as quickly as they had arrived.

I went back to Maaha, her breathing remained shallow. 'Zara, when the trolley arrives, I am going to give Maaha an injection of antibiotics into her thigh. The same place she had her immunisations done.'

Zara nodded. 'Shall I call Ishaq?'

'Yes, tell him to meet you at the hospital.'

Aiden arrived with the crash trolley. I drew up the antibiotics into a syringe. I went to Maaha, her thigh felt far too small for the needle that was about to inject her. I plunged it in, she grimaced but didn't cry.

Aiden had placed an oxygen saturation probe on Maaha's big toe. It struggled to find a reading.

'I think she is too shut down,' he said, referring to the collapse of the small blood vessels in her feet, 'it won't pick up a reading.'

He placed the oxygen mask near Maaha's face and turned it on.

The wait for the ambulance felt like forever. I was glad Aiden stayed with me because if Maaha stopped breathing I would need his help.

'Isn't there anything else you can do?' Zara pleaded.

There really wasn't, we had given her the antibiotics and now we just had to wait for an ambulance. Maaha needed blood and urine tests, x-rays and a sample of fluid from the inside of her spine to determine the source of the infection. She also needed a high dose antibiotics through a vein in her arm. None of these things could be done here at the surgery, so we just waited.

The paramedics finally arrived and made the right decision to 'scoop and run'. They realised they had a very sick baby on their hands, and without doing any kind of observations they scooped her up and took her straight to the resuscitation department at the hospital.

'You okay, mate?' Aiden asked.

'Yeah, it was just not what I was expecting,' I said, tidying up the crash trolley.

'Kids get sick really quickly,' he said. I nodded as I wheeled the trolley back down the corridor to the utility room. When I returned to my room, Aiden had left me a cup of tea on my desk.

I had to leave work on time that day, as I was meeting up with my friend Daniel. We met up every month and I was looking forward to it. We had trained to be GPs together and then, by luck, both ended up in Yorkshire. We liked to compare notes: Daniel worked in a much more affluent part of the county than I did. The two areas were worlds apart. My patients were often waiting months to be seen by a specialist, while his patients generally asked for private referrals and would usually be seen that week.

Daniel was coming over to my end, which made it a bit easier for me as the worry about Maaha and Zara had made me tired. He had texted me earlier to say he wanted to talk about something important. Daniel was already at the restaurant when I arrived.

'Is everything okay?' I asked.

'I've had a complaint,' Daniel said, looking worried.

My heart sank.

'Is it a nonsense one, or a real one?' I asked. There were complaints where the clinician had genuinely done something wrong and the best thing to do was to hold your hands up and apologise. There were other times when you had done all the right things but for some reason the patient still complained. Those were easier to respond to.

There was a case at our practice where a patient complained about the way one of our nurse practitioners had handed her a prescription. She felt it was handed over in an 'aggressive' manner. The poor nurse practitioner had no recollection of how she handed over the prescription, because it is not something you take note of. That was a nonsense complaint.

'It's a real one,' Daniel said. 'I saw a little boy last week, three years old. He came in with his mum; she said he had a bit of a temperature and cough. I examined him and checked everything. His chest was clear, and it had only been going on for a day. I told his mum it was most likely a viral infection and told her to come back if things got worse.'

'Okay,' I said. I didn't like where this story was going.

'They came back the next day and saw one of the other doctors. The cough had got worse and they were given antibiotics for it,' he said.

'Well, that isn't too bad,' I said. This wasn't an unusual story, most children with a cough and temperature do have a viral infection. And if their chest is clear it is not appropriate to give antibiotics. The clinical symptoms for children also change rapidly, and that's why we always tell parents to come back if anything changes.

'Amir, he is now in hospital with a bilateral pneumonia. He is on ITU ventilation.' Daniel took a large sip of his beer.

'Oh shit,' I said. This was a GP's worst nightmare. The reason our defence fees are so high is because we see so many patients in such a short period of time every single day. We rely on our listening and examination skills to make diagnoses. Unlike the hospital medics who have an array of instant blood tests and imaging at their fingertips and the comfort of being able to observe a patient over time, we have ten minutes. Ten minutes to make potentially life-changing decisions.

'Yes, oh shit,' Daniel echoed.

I didn't tell him about Maaha. If I had seen Maaha yesterday, chances are she would have been absolutely fine and I would have just sent her home with advice. As Aiden had said, kids get sick really quickly.

'Daniel, you saw that kid really early on in his illness. If you didn't hear anything on his chest, there was probably nothing to hear. These things can happen to any of us,' I said, trying to make him feel better. To be honest, it could have happened to any GP and I was slightly ashamed to admit that my first thought was: *Thank God it wasn't me.*

'All I keep thinking of is his little face as he sat on his mum's lap. He was smiling and really interactive. He wasn't showing any signs of a pneumonia then.'

'Who wrote in and complained?' I asked.

'His mum rang from the hospital. Our practice manager told me today. I offered to ring the mum back but she said she didn't want to talk to me.'

'I'm sorry, Daniel,' I said. 'What are you going to do?'

'Not much I can do, let's just hope he gets better.' He took a sip of his beer.

'I am sure he will. Children are resilient.' I said. The waitress came and took our order and I tried to move the conversation on. I knew how heavily the complaint would be weighing on his mind all evening. And I knew how much Daniel would be worrying about the little boy. You can't switch off your emotions when your day's surgery finishes; you can't help being caught up in your patients' outcomes.

*

Friday morning, and I arrived at the practice as usual. I normally arrive an hour before my clinic starts to get ahead. I like to have a strong coffee and action my patients' blood results and hospital letters. Once I've done that, I sit with my colleagues and we have a bit of gossip and catch-up. This morning was different. I rang the hospital to find out what had happened to Maaha, nobody answered on the ward. They must be busy, I thought.

As always, my clinic filled up with patients soon after the phone lines opened. It was going to be another busy day. Just after 10 a.m. I got a call from reception.

'Hi Amir, it's Sandra.' Sandra was one of receptionists, she was a real character. When I first started at the surgery I didn't know what to make of her; she seemed to be in a constant state of stress and on the verge of tears but it was never quite clear why. Yet she was always so good and helpful with patients.

'Hi Sandra,' I replied.

'I have Zara Sinha on the phone. She wants to come and see you but you're full. She said it was urgent.'

That was good news. If Zara could come to see me at the surgery it meant she didn't have to be at the hospital and Maaha was doing well. 'Oh that's fine, just tell her to come at the end of my clinic. She did say she would drop in today.'

'Okay,' Sandra said hesitantly. 'I'll add her to the bottom of your list.'

My morning clinic normally finishes at midday. Zara had been booked in at 12 p.m. and the computer told me she had arrived a few minutes early. I finished with my last patient and buzzed her in. It had been a busy morning, but I was keen to find out how Maaha was doing.

Chapter 6

There was a knock on the door.

'Come in,' I said, getting up out of my chair and opening the door.

Zara stood in the corridor with Ishaq. She was wearing a grey shawl that was wrapped around her several times. Ishaq, who normally wore carefully ironed shirts and pressed trousers, stood in a pair of sweatpants and a white t-shirt.

'My baby is dead,' Zara said quietly. She wasn't crying, there was no emotion in her voice. She stood in the corridor.

'Come in,' I said quietly. Neither of them moved. 'Please, come in.' I said a bit louder this time. I suddenly felt like the wind had been knocked out of me. It wasn't the news I had expected.

I remember thinking that I had had years of training in dealing with patients and the range of issues they come in with. I recalled thinking back to the two days we had in medical school where we were taught about death and caring for dying patients and their families. It didn't matter; nothing I had been taught over the last fifteen years seemed relevant to this situation.

She repeated her words, this time in a whisper: 'My baby is dead.'

Ishaq spoke next. 'We came straight from the hospital. We couldn't face going home.'

I led them to the chairs and sat them down.

'Do you want to tell me about what happened?' I asked. 'You don't have to, only if it will help.'

Zara wasn't looking at me, she was staring at something behind me, something that wasn't there. Her face looked different, as though it was being pulled down by some unseen weight. I let the silence hang in the air, I didn't want them to feel they had to re-live whatever had happened if they didn't want to. I also didn't know what the right thing to say was. I couldn't think of anything worse than losing a baby, and it had only happened a few hours ago.

I imagine people think doctors will always know what to do in these circumstances. In hospitals, when children die there are specially trained nurses and bereavement officers who speak to the parents. They deal with this on a regular basis and I imagine they have set words and phrases in their arsenal that are appropriate to these situations.

Eventually Ishaq broke the silence.

'The doctor said she had a serious infection, maybe meningitis. They are still waiting for some of the tests to come back,' he gulped.

'Would you like a glass of water?' I asked.

He nodded.

I messaged Sandra who brought in two glasses of water and placed them on the table. Ishaq took his and drank. Zara didn't look up.

I didn't say anything.

'They said she was really sick and the infection had taken over her body. There were lots of doctors and nurses there in the Emergency Department. They kept putting needles in her. It was horrible,' Ishaq's voice broke.

'You don't have to tell me,' I said, passing him a tissue.

'She died this morning, just after 4 a.m.,' Zara said. 'Sepsis, that's what the nurse said.'

Ishaq put his hand on her knee, she didn't move.

'I am so sorry,' I said, feeling feeble. 'Babies of this age, they get sick so quickly.'

'Zara,' I said, 'there is nothing you could have done that would have changed this. This is not your fault.' I knew she could probably see the tears building in my eyes, but I didn't care. 'Nobody could have predicted this, it's just the most awful of things and I am so sorry it has happened to you.'

'Maybe if I had noticed she was unwell sooner. Maybe if I had brought her to see you in the morning when I first noticed she wasn't feeding properly. I just didn't want to be one of those neurotic first-time mums.'

'Zara, listen to me,' I said firmly. 'This is not your fault. This is the worst thing that could ever have happened to you, but you did not cause this. It's just a terrible, terrible tragedy.' Zara continued to stare into space. Ishaq was now too looking at the same spot.

'Listen to me,' I continued, 'this is going to be a difficult time for you. You are going to have trouble sleeping, eating and you will have some very dark thoughts, but there is help and you must talk to me or someone else about your feelings.'

'Thank you,' Ishaq said, looking up.

We talked for a while longer. The hospital child bereavement team were visiting her tomorrow. They would help her sort out the nursery and all the baby clothes. I arranged to see them again on Monday.

'The doctor at the hospital said you could give me a tablet to stop me making breast milk,' Zara said before she left. 'I've been making it for the last day and I really want it to stop.'

It was one of the cruellest things; even after a baby has died, mums still produce breast milk. The maternal hormones are all still there, circulating around, and the body carries on as if nothing has happened. But something had happened.

'Of course,' I said, grateful to be able to do something for her.

When they left, I sat in my chair and stared at the computer screen. I didn't know if I had helped her in any way. I knew she was going home to a house full of baby toys and clothes but no baby. I couldn't think of anything worse.

There isn't a word for a mum who has lost her child. When a woman loses her husband she is a widow, when you lose your parents you are orphaned. But what if you lose your child? Is it that it's just so sad that nobody could think of a word to do it justice? Or is it that nobody wants a word that describes such a tragic situation to blemish their language?

I thought about what would have happened if I had not been in today, if Zara and Ishaq had seen another GP and had had to tell her story to someone who didn't know them. I wasn't family, but I was someone they trusted, and that trust had been gained through multiple consultations and time.

I knew this sadness would live with them in some form forever. I would always be acutely aware of it every time I saw either of them. Our relationship changed from that day. There was an understanding between us; I had been an outsider who had shared the most private and tragic part of their life.

A few years have passed since this happened. I still see Zara and Ishaq, though not as much. They are trying for another baby but have not yet been successful, and as each year passes and they get older those chances become slimmer and slimmer.

Each time she sees me, before she leaves my room, Zara always says the same thing to me:

'Pray for us, Dr Khan, pray we have another baby.'

Chapter Seven

I had reached a stalemate with my patient. We stared at each other. I couldn't give him what he wanted and he appeared to not want to leave until I did. We were at an impasse.

'Mr James, your chest is absolutely clear. Your temperature is fine and your throat is mildly inflamed. All of this point to you having a viral infection. These things usually resolve on their own. Antibiotics won't work,' I said for the third time.

'But I know I have a chest infection. I've been coughing for two weeks,' he said matter-of-factly.

'Coughs from viral infections can last up to three weeks,' I said. I wasn't giving in. We have a huge antibiotic resistance crisis on our hands around the world and, sadly, GPs are being scape-goated as the cause for it, never mind the huge amounts of antibiotics used in the farming industry, or the fact that in many countries antibiotics are available without a prescription over the counter. But, of course, the common perception it is us GPs who are the cause for the antibiotic crisis with our willy-nilly prescribing.

'What if I get pneumonia? You'll be sorry then,' Mr James said.

'I will be surprised rather than sorry if you get pneumonia, Mr James,' I said, turning back to my computer. Turning away was a tactic I used to signal to a patient the consultation was over.

'I want to see another GP. I want a second opinion,' he said. Every patient in the NHS is entitled to a second opinion if they want one, and a lot of the time I am understanding of this, but I wasn't today. Giving Mr James an appointment with another GP today for his sore throat would mean another patient would not get seen.

'You're more than welcome to come back if things don't improve over the next week.' I had already started writing up my notes.

'I want a second opinion today,' he said.

'Mr James, I am sorry but I can't imagine any GP in this building giving you antibiotics for a viral infection. They simply will not work. Besides, there are no more appointments left for today.'

'Well, I am not leaving until I see another doctor.' Mr James sat back in his chair and folded his arms defiantly.

I pondered the situation for a moment. I saved my notes, switched off my computer and packed up my things.

'In that case, I will leave.' I left him alone in the room. Walking into reception I asked which rooms were free.

'You can have room nine,' Nicola called out across the room.

'Thanks, Nicola. Also there is a patient in room four who is refusing to leave, can you let Gerard know?'

'I'm on it,' Nicola said. The fact that she didn't ask any questions showed how often these kinds of things took place. Gerard was our caretaker. He usually handled situations like this well. I set up shop in room nine, mentally preparing my response to Mr James's inevitable written complaint.

Zero tolerance. That is the policy in the NHS towards abusive behaviour from patients.

88

Chapter 7

You see the posters in almost every NHS establishment you visit, a selection of photographs of NHS employees with a black eye, a bust lip or a broken nose looking directly at you, with text stating these are genuine injuries sustained from patients.

I always wondered if they really were genuine NHS workers whenever I saw that poster, or perhaps they are just models who were being used to represent what had happened to NHS workers. Either way, it's pretty horrific.

Every healthcare worker will have a story about being verbally or physically abused by a patient. It's just part and parcel of working in the NHS. It shouldn't be, but it is. There is always an excuse – maybe the patient was frustrated or they were very unwell and that's why they behaved that way; we must be more understanding of the reasons.

Zero tolerance rarely means zero tolerance when it comes to the NHS. I think a more accurate description of the policy would be: well, let's give them one more chance, it was the staff member's fault really.

I remember my first incident of being verbally abused in the NHS. It came shortly after I qualified as a doctor, during my time as trainee GP. I had a great training experience in a small practice in the middle of an affluent village.

It was lovely village and the surgery I was based in was one of those small family practices where the receptionists know every patient by their first names as they come in. It was very white, very middle class, and there weren't very many brown people there. Whenever I was doing a surgery, the patients would walk in and give me a surprised look as if to say, 'I wasn't expecting you today. Where is nice Dr Kenny?' Although they generally warmed to me by the end of the consultation, I invariably had the same conversation every day with a different patient:

'So doctor, you're not from around here, where are you from?'

'Oh yes, you're right, Mrs Wattle. I am from Yorkshire.'

'Yes, but where are you from?' Mrs Wattle would press.

'Well, I grew up in Bradford,' I would say slowly so she could understand. Perhaps it was my Yorkshire accent.

'I see, but where are you from originally?'

'I was born in Bradford, West Yorkshire, Mrs Wattle,' I would say, slightly confused.

'And are your parents from Bradford?' Mrs Wattle would ask, clearly dissatisfied with my first three answers.

Here we go, she wanted to know my country of origin – why the hell didn't she just say that in the first place? I mean, it wasn't an offensive question, although I had no idea what difference it would make to the treatment of her haemorrhoids.

'My dad was from India and my mum is from Pakistan,' I would reply. That seemed to satisfy her. She would sit back in her chair, interrogation complete. Now she could apply her haemorrhoid creams safe in the knowledge I was of true South Asian heritage.

It turns out Mrs Wattle hadn't finished. 'Do you know Deepak from the newsagents in the village? He is from India too.'

None of these conversations really bothered me, though when I played them back to my Caucasian friends over dinner they were hugely offended on my behalf and refer to it as 'casual racism'. *Bloody hell*, I would think, *if they think that's offensive, I'd better not tell them of the actual racist abuse I get!*

I was on a home visit. A GP's day is usually split into a morning clinic, followed by home visits, then an afternoon or evening clinic.

Chapter 7

When I tell people now that I go on house calls to see patients they seem genuinely surprised that doctors still make them. We never stopped, but we are reasonably strict about who is eligible. The patient really does have to be housebound due to an illness to qualify for such a visit, not because they would simply prefer for the doctor to come to them, rather than they come to us.

One of the community midwives had rung up earlier to say that a lady who had recently had a baby via a caesarean section was possibly septic from an infection in her surgical wound site. She couldn't come to the surgery as she was too unwell, and the baby had also spent time in the special care baby unit and was still recovering. It seemed like a reasonable visit request.

Once morning surgery was over, I gathered my things and put them into my doctor's bag. It was one of those small villages where you could walk most places, so I printed off a map and headed out.

You're never quite sure what you are going to find when you go on a house call. Often the houses can look perfectly normal on the outside but the patient could be living in complete squalor on the inside. Other times, I had visited patients in the poorest parts, but when I got inside they had a better state-of-the-art plasma television with surround sound than me.

There is always a slight trepidation when visiting a patient at home. The tables are turned. This is their territory and their rules, as opposed to the surgery which is my territory and my rules.

I found my way to a nondescript-looking terraced house and knocked on the door. Immediately, there was the sound of a dog barking.

'STOP IT, LEO!' a voice called from inside. 'It's just the doctor.' Leo didn't stop; he continued to bark loudly and throw himself against the door. *Great*, I thought, *I'm about to get attacked by a rabid dog.* The sound of the keys turning in the doorway pulled me out of my thoughts and the door opened.

'Don't worry, he doesn't bite,' a lady in her late twenties said as she opened the door. Leo growled behind her and gave another bark.

'Hi, is it Mrs Hanson?' I asked, keeping one eye on Leo.

'No that's my sister, she's inside.' She held the door open to let me in. I carefully manoeuvred myself around Leo, trying not to look too scared. *They can smell fear*, I told myself. *Act casual.*

I was led into the living room where the curtains were still drawn. There were children's toys strewn across the floor and I had to concentrate hard not to fall over them in the dark. The TV was the only source of light in the room. Mrs Hanson was laid on the sofa watching *Loose Women*. They were discussing whether a particular celebrity's latest video, which involved her prancing around in her underwear eating hot dogs in a seductive way, was empowering or demeaning to women.

'I think she looks lovely, and if that's what makes her feel good, she should do it,' Coleen Nolan said. 'If I looked like that, I'd never wear clothes.'

'Yes, but think about the message she is sending out to all those impressionable young girls out there,' Janet Street-Porter replied.

Helena Hanson hadn't noticed I had entered the room; she was so engrossed. I coughed to signal my presence. She startled.

'Fuck, I didn't see you there, sorry,' she said.

I smiled. 'Hi, I'm Dr Khan. Are you Mrs Hanson?'

Chapter 7

'Helena, and yes I am.' Helena tried to sit up, but immediately winced, holding her stomach.

'It's okay, Helena, just stay where you are.' The noise had woken up the baby who had been sleeping silently in his basket by the side of the sofa. Helena sat upright and picked him up. The Loose Women were still talking in the background.

'Do you mind if we turn the TV down?' I asked. Helena nodded and switched the TV off, plunging the room into darkness. She immediately switched on a lamp. It was the middle of the afternoon but it felt like the depths of the night in this living room.

I sat down. 'I understand you haven't been feeling well, Helena,' I started.

The baby was still crying. 'I am just going to feed him while we talk,' Helena said, wincing from the movement of unbuttoning her pyjama top while holding the baby. The baby immediately latched on to Helena's breast and guzzled happily.

'Have you had increased pain from your scar sitc?' I continued.

'Yes, it's been ten days now but it feels worse today than it did the day I had my surgery,' she said softly, glancing down at her feeding baby. There is something special about the connection between a mother and her new-born child and it was gratifying to know that, despite Helena having a traumatic birth and a subsequent caesarean section, she had still bonded with her son and he was her top priority. Biology was amazing like that.

'Have you had a temperature or noticed any pus or redness from around your wound site?' I said, breaking away from my thoughts.

'Yes, I felt really hot last night and my wound is looking really swollen.'

'Okay, well, when you are ready, can I take a look at the wound?' I unclasped my bag and took out my gloves and thermometer. The baby had fallen back asleep, so Helena placed him back in his basket, careful not to wake him. She slowly positioned herself back on the sofa and lay down.

I got up to examine her. As I did I heard the thud thud thud of someone running down the corridor outside and the living room door flung open. A young boy aged around seven bounded in, stopping as he saw me.

'This is my other son, Angus,' Helena said. 'Angus, say hello to the doctor.'

Angus didn't say anything. He rushed over to his mum and nestled his head in her neck. To my surprise, he then lifted up her T-shirt and attached himself to her breast and started drinking.

I watched as Angus, a seven-year-old child, breastfed from his mother. Now, I am an advocate for breastfeeding and feel very strongly that breast milk is best for babies, provided it's the mother's choice to breastfeed, but this didn't feel right to me.

'Isn't he a bit too old to be breastfed?' I asked gingerly.

Helena looked at me and was about to answer, but before she could, Angus took himself off her breast and answered for her.

'Why don't you fuck off?' he said, before turning his head around and drinking from his mother's bosom again.

I gasped audibly. Had this seven-year-old child really just told me to fuck off? I couldn't quite believe it. Here he was, drinking milk from his mother's breast like butter wouldn't melt, and he had just sworn at me to my face. I had to say something.

'Well, I think if he is old enough to tell me to "fuck off" then he is old enough to drink from a cup!' I said. Normally, I am one of those people who comes away from a heated discussion wishing I had thought of a million clever things to say, but this time I was rather pleased with my reply.

'I am so sorry,' Helena said, pulling Angus off her breast. 'I don't know why he would have said that. He never normally swears. Angus, say sorry to this nice doctor.'

Angus pulled himself out of his mother's grip and ran out of the room, without saying a word. Helena looked too embarrassed for me to make a big deal of it. I examined her wound and agreed it looked infected. I told her I would leave a prescription for some antibiotics for her sister to collect from the surgery and left.

That was it. I had been verbally abused for the first time in my medical career. Should I send Angus a zero tolerance letter, detailing our practice's policy of not allowing this kind of behaviour towards our employees? *No*, I thought, *I'll give him one more chance, it was my fault really.*

Angus and I saw each other one more time after this. His mum brought him to the surgery with a cough. We both eyed each other rather suspiciously. I was careful not to upset him; I didn't want to face his wrath again. Thankfully, he was perfectly behaved.

As they were leaving, him mum said to him, 'Say thank you to the nice doctor, Angus.'

Angus looked at me stubbornly. 'Angus?' his mum said again.

'Thank you, doctor,' Angus mumbled.

His mum looked simultaneously relieved and proud. Well, it certainly was an improvement from being sworn at, I thought.

'You are very welcome, Angus,' I said, and I was rather proud of myself for getting one over on him.

After I had had my first taste of abuse from Angus, I went on to have several more as my career unfolded. I wasn't alone, in fact I have had discussions with my colleagues on a weekly basis about incidents where they have been victim to intimidating behaviour. Unlike the incident with Angus, when an adult patient starts to shout and swear at you it can be a scary experience and leaves you feeling very unsettled.

When you think about it, GPs put themselves in vulnerable positions every day. They are alone in a room with a stranger and anything could happen. If that stranger decides they are having a really bad day and wants to pull out a knife and stab their doctor, there is very little that we can do about it. Similarly, when we go out on house calls, we are doing so in good faith but in reality we are entering the complete unknown. Anything could be waiting for us behind closed doors. To be fair, truly violent incidents are rare, but they are not unheard of. There have been well-documented cases of doctors being violently beaten and even killed by their patients. People often ask me why patients have to walk around me to the far side of the room to sit down for their consultation, rather than sit by the door they enter from. The reason is that, if things take a nasty turn, the patient can't block my exit from the room. These are the things we have to think about when deciding on the layout of our consulting rooms.

Thursday afternoon and my day was nearly over. The day hadn't started well; I had forgotten my lunch bag at home. I had made sandwiches to eat at work and left them on the kitchen counter. I could imagine them getting soggy and warm as the sunlight came in through the window. They would have to be thrown away when I got back. More seriously, I had also had a particularly challenging consultation in the morning that involved telling a patient their chest x-ray had come back suggestive of cancer. It had taken more than the allocated ten minutes, which meant I had been running late the rest of the morning. I had to apologise to each patient for their wait as they came in. Some of them grumbled about it, as if it were my fault that I had had the audacity to spend a bit more time with the patient with lung cancer so that I could explain the next steps carefully and sensitively. I was not in a good mood, but it was okay: the day was nearly over.

I called in my next patient, a 23-year-old man called Zadenko Taklova. The appointment note said he was coming in to talk about his knee pain. I quickly scanned through his records before he entered – he had seen one of my colleagues two months ago with knee pain, her examination of the knee had been normal and she had referred him to see a physiotherapist. I looked in the letters to see he had not attended his physio appointment, despite them writing to him twice, and he had been subsequently discharged.

He came in without knocking, walked around me and sat down on the chair. There didn't seem to be anything wrong with his knee as he walked in.

'Hi, I'm Dr Khan, how can I help?'

'I want you to write me a letter,' he said. There was something about him that I didn't like. He was cocky. I put that thought to the back of my mind; I was just in a bad mood and I wasn't being fair to him.

'Okay, well, this is the first time we have met so do you mind telling me why you would like me to write you a letter?'

'Yeah, it's my knee, it's still hurting, and they want me to go to court tomorrow and I want you to write me a letter to say that I can't go to court because of my knee.' Zadenko kept moving around in his chair, but didn't break eye contact with me.

I learned about the importance of eye contact in a doctor's consultation when I was in medical school. It is important to maintain eye contact to establish a rapport and trust, but too much eye contact could be deemed intimidating. I broke my gaze from Zadenko and looked at my computer.

'I can see you came to see one of my colleagues about your knee and she referred you for physiotherapy?' I asked.

'Yeah, that didn't work, it still hurts so I want that letter for tomorrow.'

'But we have had a letter from the physiotherapy department saying you didn't attend the appointment, Mr Taklova.'

'I never got no letter from them.'

'Well, they have posted it to your home address twice. Anyway, never mind that, why don't you tell me about your knee and I can assess it?' I said, knowing it would be futile to pursue the physiotherapy appointment.

He pointed to the front of his knee. 'It hurts here when I stand for too long.'

'How long is "too long"?' I asked.

'I dunno, maybe twenty minutes,' he said. 'Look, are you going to do me this letter? I need it for tomorrow.' Zadenko was getting agitated, he began to move around in his seat more and kept looking at his phone.

'Do you take any painkillers to help with the pain?'

Zadenko shook his head.

'Perhaps I can examine your knee and afterwards we can talk about the letter,' I said. He pulled up his trouser leg and I knelt down to examine the knee. It looked and felt perfectly fine, no swelling, no give in the ligaments and no signs of injury. 'Did anything happen to make your knee hurt?' I enquired as I examined him.

Zadenko shrugged, more interested in his phone than what was going on in the room. He was typing out a text message to someone. I sat back down in my chair.

Chapter 7

'Mr Taklova, the good news is that my examination of your knee is normal, so I don't think there is anything serious going on. If your knee has been hurting for the last two months, I could refer you back to see the physiotherapist, but you will have to try to attend this time,' I said.

'I don't want to see no physiotherapist; I want you to write me a letter for court tomorrow. You're not listening to me.' Zadenko was becoming visibly angry and he spat the last sentence out with a snarl. I could feel a slight nervousness in the pit of my stomach.

'Mr Taklova, it doesn't really work like that. I don't feel I have any medical reason to state you cannot attend court tomorrow, and even if I did, letters like this can take up to five working days to process.' I knew this would upset him further but I wasn't prepared to put my signature on a letter that I didn't believe in. This chap's knee seemed fine to me. He had missed his physiotherapy appointment, he didn't require any pain relief and the examination was normal, so there was no reason he couldn't attend court tomorrow.

'I need that fucking letter today,' Zadenko said, deliberately and slowly. He had stopped fidgeting and put his phone back in his pocket. He now gave me his full, undivided attention.

'Do you mind me asking why you are in court tomorrow?' I asked, thinking a different line of questioning might diffuse the situation.

'That's nothing to do with you. All I want from you is a letter saying I can't go to court due to health reasons.'

I had had enough of this consultation. Zadenko was giving me a very bad feeling and I wanted him out of the room.

'Our practice policy is that any requests for letters need to be put in writing by the patient and there is a charge for them ...'

'I couldn't give a fuck about your practice policy,' Zadenko said, standing up, 'you're just a GP, and if I want you to write me a letter you're going to write me a fucking letter.' Zadenko took a step closer, standing directly over me.

I stood up too, meeting his gaze. I walked slowly towards the door and opened it. 'This consultation is over, Mr Taklova, and I would like you to leave,' I said. I admit I was scared. Zadenko was much bigger than me, and the fact that he was going to court tomorrow suggested he had a criminal past, probably violent. I wanted him out.

He didn't move.

'I am not leaving this surgery until you give me that letter,' he said. Zadenko was getting louder now. A patient walked past in the corridor and looked in but kept walking.

'If you don't leave now, Mr Taklova, I will call the police,' I said loudly. I was hoping another member of staff would hear the conversation. We do have a panic button in our room that alerts every staff member to an emergency, but it was under my desk and Zadenko was now standing right by it.

'So call the police. I know you, Amir. I know which car you drive. You think you're all big working in this surgery. I'll be waiting for you. I'll be waiting for you and I am going to fuck you up.' Zadenko grinned and stared at me. After a pause, he walked out.

I let out a breath. He had called me by my first name, which had been unsettlingly familiar. I could feel my heart racing, I was shaking and feeling slightly nauseous. I hadn't ever been threatened like that before; this was a new experience. I stood by the door for a minute, not knowing what to do. I wanted to tell someone about what had happened, but I had two more patients to see and I was now running even more late.

Chapter 7

I decided I needed to talk to someone about what had just happened. I couldn't see my next patient straight away; I wouldn't be able to focus properly. My head was still full of the vile things Zadenko had said to me.

I went into reception and found our manager, Nicola. I told her what had happened, omitting the part where I felt like I was going to pass out after he left. I was worried he would come good on his threat of waiting for me in the car park and we both thought it best to call the police.

I think what people forget, when they decide to get angry or shout at their doctor for whatever reason, is that the doctor cannot just take a breather or go home because they have been upset. They have no gaps in their clinics: patients are booked in at ten-minute intervals and there is no space to process your own emotions. You have to box them off and give yourself to the next patient. After I spoke with Nicola, I went back to my room and called in my next patient. It was a lovely old man but I found it hard to listen to him when I talked, as my mind kept going back to the previous consult.

I had come to work that day with the sole purpose to help people, so it didn't feel fair that someone could come in and make me feel intimidated. I was also a bit disappointed in myself for letting Zadenko upset me so much and ruin my subsequent consultation; this poor old man deserved my full attention yet I was unable to give it to him.

I had to stay late that day in surgery in order to give a statement to the police. It was a young officer who wrote down everything I said, word for word. He told me what Zadenko had done would be classed as an assault. I was surprised, as he hadn't hit me. The officer told me that if he had hit me then that would be battery, but his threatening behaviour amounted to assault.

They would pay him a visit tonight and the policeman asked if I wanted to press charges.

I wasn't sure. It felt a bit much to press charges – I just wanted him to get a slap on the wrist and to never do it again. The police officer suggested I really thought about following through with it, and told me that a 'slap on the wrist' rarely works on these kinds of people. I said I would think about it.

He walked me to my car, which was embarrassing but I was kind of glad of it. Zadenko wasn't there, which made me feel even more ashamed. I was constantly telling my male patients that it was okay to feel low or emotional, but here I was embarrassed by my need to be walked to my car by a police officer.

I couldn't stop thinking about that consultation all night, it kept me awake. I thought about it again while I was out running before work the next day. Could I have done anything differently? Had the fact that I had not been in the best mood that day affected the consultation? It took days for me to get over it and I talked about it many times with my colleagues, who were all very supportive.

I did decide to press charges in the end, with the agreement that the statement the police officer had taken from me would suffice. It turned out Zadenko was in court for assault; he was clearly someone who was well versed in using intimidating behaviour. The police officer told me they would enter my statement as additional evidence against him.

A couple of months later, on a Saturday morning, I came home from doing the grocery shop. There was a letter waiting for me in our mailbox. I opened it while unpacking my bags. It was from the Criminal Justice Courts. The letter told me how the courts liked to inform victims of abuse about the sentences their abusers had received. I hadn't really thought of myself as a 'victim' of any sort. But there it was in black and white. Zadenko had received a six-week prison sentence.

I wasn't sure how to feel. I imagine that sentence was also the result of other crimes he had committed as well as a result of his behaviour towards me. I certainly didn't have any feelings of satisfaction – I don't think any healthcare professional would want this outcome for one of their patients, no matter how badly they had behaved. I had to keep reminding myself I had done nothing wrong and I was not responsible for him going to prison: he was. It was hard to think of it that way.

When you are training to be a doctor, you are shown how to deal with consultations where you have to break bad news or manage desperately sad situations. There is an expectation that you can do this and do it well. But nobody prepares you for how you feel when you have been abused, assaulted or shouted at by patients. That is a whole new set of emotions that we deal with quietly on our own.

Abuse from patients is still rife in the NHS, and it is not uncommon for an incident similar to this to occur once a month in our practice alone. A doctor I know was found crying in a bathroom one time when a patient refused to leave her room after a particularly bad consultation. She had been discovered by one of the reception staff when they came to investigate why her next patient had been waiting for over an hour to be seen.

One of the nicest doctors I have ever met had his car vandalised in our car park with horrible racist abuse by a patient who was later arrested.

If I am being honest, there is still a part of me that remains cautious when going out into the car park. Zadenko will have been released from prison now (unless, of course his sentence was extended for bad behaviour, which wouldn't surprise me) and I am still working at the same surgery. There is nothing to stop him walking into my room and picking up where he left off.

I hope he doesn't, but in case he does I am now very familiar with how to use my panic button.

I was seeing Daniel again the evening after the Zadenko incident. I was going to reschedule after what had happened that day but he sounded upset on the phone. I told him I would drive to York to see him.

The little boy who had been admitted to hospital with bilateral pneumonia had sadly died. Daniel had already had two beers before I got there.

'Daniel, have you driven here?' I asked.

'Taxi,' he replied and took another glug.

'Okay, good.' I sat down opposite him. He looked terrible. His eyes were bloodshot and had dark circles underneath them. His hair needed a wash and he hadn't shaved. 'You look like shit, mate.'

'Jesus, it's nice to see you too. I'm off work, I don't need to make an effort,' he said.

'What do you mean you're "off work"?' I asked.

'I needed some time off work. Went to see my GP, "stress-related problem" he put on the sick note,' Daniel replied.

Stress-related problem was something GPs often put on sick notes. It covered a whole array of possibilities, from work stress to a relative being sick in hospital. It was highly unusual for a GP to see another GP in this capacity, as there is a tendency to 'soldier on'. It is an idiotic tendency, of course.

'I tried going back to work and seeing patients but I just couldn't concentrate on anything they were saying. I couldn't afford to make another mistake like I did with that kid, so I'm

Chapter 7

off.' He raised his glass in a mock 'cheers' and finished his drink. 'So now I can drink on a school night.'

'Probably not your finest decision, Daniel,' I said. The waitress came round, having clocked Daniel's empty glass, and asked if we wanted more drinks. 'A jug of water and two glasses, please,' I said sharply to her. She got the hint.

'Daniel, what's going on with the family? Have you heard from them?' As hard as this was for Daniel, it would be much worse for the poor family who had lost their son.

'They've put in a formal complaint. My defence union is dealing with it, we've sent them all the notes,' he said, looking out of the window at some people getting out of their car. 'There's most likely going to be a coroner's inquest. I'm not sure.'

'Okay, well there isn't anything you can do at the moment,' I said.

Daniel looked back at me, tears in his eyes. 'I let that family down, Amir. They came to see me with their little boy and I let them down and now he is dead.'

I shook my head, lost for words.

'Daniel, do you think you would do anything differently if you saw him again?' I asked.

'That's the thing, I am not sure I would,' he said flatly.

After we finished eating, I offered to drive Daniel home. I could only imagine what he was going through. For all the abusive patients I have had to deal with in my time, there is nothing worse than the feeling that you have let someone down. The grief you give yourself is much harder to bear than the grief anyone else can give you. We are always our own harshest critics.

Chapter Eight

I understand empty nest syndrome, that feeling when someone with whom you have a close relationship decides it's time to spread their wings and leave the comfort of their usual place of dwelling. Sometimes, as the responsible adult, you think that they're not quite ready but you let them go anyway, and they surprise you. Other times your worries are justified.

This is how I feel about my GP trainees every summer. By this time, I have a spent a year nurturing them, advising them on how to consult with patients, supporting them when they receive their first complaint, picking them up and dusting them off if they fail an exam. Then summer comes and they are fully fledged, and off they pop to surgeries far and wide.

When most people have visions of chicks growing up and leaving a nest, I imagine they think of fluffy cutesy birds taking tentative steps along a branch and unfolding their wings timidly, bouncing on the spot and then whoosh, off they go. In my head it's slightly different. I remember seeing a nature documentary about a family of merganser ducks that were nesting in a tree cavity. To fledge, the ducklings had to jump out of the hole one by one and fall fifty feet to the floor. They didn't fly, they just fell. Once on the floor, they would look a bit dazed then waddle off to find their parents. What kind of parents would allow this?

I think of my trainees leaving for another practice like this – jumping from a height into the great unknown. What if they don't enjoy it at the new practice? What if someone is mean to them? I know they can't all stay at our surgery but it would be nice if they could.

We are trained to be GP trainers, but all the training in the world cannot prepare you for every outcome.

Of course, I get the occasional trainee who I am secretly pleased to see the back of (I am only human), but by and large it is a positive experience. Sometimes a trainee sticks in your mind for other reasons, though, and you find yourself wondering what will become of them.

It was one of those rainy mornings where you have to run to your car, and although its only ten yards away you end up soaked and dishevelled. Then you get to work and have the pleasure of running from your car to the surgery, and the intensity of the rain has doubled since you left the house.

I took off my coat which was heavy from the rain and hung it up, hoping it would be dry by lunchtime. The computer whirred to life and I nipped to the kitchen to prepare my morning coffee. I am normally the first person in at work. I like being the only person there and the quiet that brings.

I went to the kitchen and was surprised to see Charlotte, one of our nurses, sitting at the table and sipping nervously at her cup of tea.

'Oh, hi Charlotte,' I said. 'You're here early.' I opened up the cupboard in an attempt to find a clean cup. The kitchen was adorned with posters encouraging staff to wash, dry and put away their own cups, but despite this the sink was brimming with dirty cups from the night before.

'Hi Amir, how are you?' Charlotte asked, not making eye contact with me.

'I'd be better if it wasn't raining so much. Do you think it'll keep the patients away?'

'Doubt it,' Charlotte said flatly.

Charlotte was one of our newer nurses; she had come to us as a student and had stayed on after she qualified. She had been with us for about six months and was progressing well. Both staff and patients liked her and she was always eager to help when things got tough. The only thing I really knew about Charlotte was that she had recently been proposed to by her boyfriend on a hot air balloon which had caused quite a commotion in reception. She was now busy planning what sounded like a very extravagant wedding.

'Yeah, you're probably right,' I said. Having found a relatively clean cup I was now searching for a spoon that didn't have a brown stain in the middle of it.

'Actually, Amir, I came in early to speak to you. In confidence, if you don't mind.'

I looked at her a bit uncertainly. I knew Charlotte fairly well but I didn't really have a lot to do with her. The nurses were managed by one of our other GPs, Marcus Daniels, so it was unusual that they would come directly to me with any issues.

'Sure, no problem. Do you want to talk here or in my room?' I asked.

'Your room would be better.'

I gave up on finding a clean spoon and picked up a used one. I gave it a quick run over with boiling water and hoped for the best. *What doesn't kill you makes you stronger (or gives you the shits)*, I thought. We walked back to my room and sat down.

Charlotte's eyes were flitting nervously around the room. They eventually settled and she unzipped her handbag and pulled out her phone. She held on to it and didn't say anything.

'Is everything okay, Charlotte?' I asked. To be honest I was feeling a bit bewildered. It was still only 7 a.m. and by now I had usually drunk a cup of coffee and was halfway through my paper-work. I was beginning to wish Charlotte would just say whatever it was she wanted to say.

'Um, not really. This is really difficult because I know he is your trainee, but I've had a few issues with Andrew.' She held out her phone and gestured that I should look at the screen.

Andrew Goddard was my GP trainee. He was coming up to his eighth month with us and already he had passed his exams and was performing well. Initially shy, Andy had eventually set-tled and was flourishing. He was never going to be the life and soul of the party but he worked hard and had made a place for himself at the surgery.

'Andy?' I said, taking the phone from her. 'What's happened?'

'That is a text he wrote me. It might be easier if you just read it.'

I gave Charlotte one final look before turning my attention to the screen. It was from Andy's number, which I also had saved on my phone. As I read it, my eyes widened and I felt sick in the pit of my stomach.

The text detailed very passionate feelings that Andy had been harbouring for Charlotte. It went on to describe how he thought about her all day, and how much he looked forward to seeing her at work. It then said she was making the biggest mistake of her life marrying a man who didn't love her as much as Andy did. It ended with Andy saying he knew it would be tough breaking off an engagement, but he knew it was for the best and he sensed she did too.

I felt like I had walked into some parallel workplace. I had arrived this morning with the most worrying thing on my mind being my hair being ruined in the rain, and now I seemed to have become embroiled in some workplace love scandal. It was exactly the kind of situation I spent my entire life trying to avoid. I wasn't quite sure what to say.

'I'm sorry, Charlotte, I'm a bit lost for words. I wasn't expecting to be reading a love text at this time in the morning,' I said honestly. For heaven's sake, I hadn't even had a sip of my coffee yet.

'I am sorry to put it on you, but Michelle said to come and speak with you about it. She said as you were his mentor you could deal with it.' Michelle was our lead nurse; she was who Charlotte reported directly to before Marcus got involved.

'No, you did the right thing,' I said, suddenly feeling very sorry for Charlotte. 'How are you feeling about this? Has he said anything to you, or made you feel uncomfortable in any way?'

'No, no, absolutely not, this text came as a complete surprise to be honest. I thought we had a bit of banter but that's about it. I didn't know he had any romantic feelings for me.'

I couldn't imagine Andy having 'banter' with anyone. It was difficult to get him to talk about anything but work.

'Okay, well I'll talk to him. It's important he understands this is not appropriate behaviour. How far do you want me to escalate this?' I asked.

'I just want him to know that I am happily engaged and that any feelings he has for me are unfounded and not reciprocated.'

'Okay, leave it with me. Could you please send me a screenshot of the message?' After more discussion, Charlotte was satisfied the situation would be resolved. She left the room and I went back to sipping my now-cold coffee. I didn't dare go back to the kitchen for fear of bumping into another drama.

I rested my elbows on the table and put my face into my hands. This was going to be tricky. Andy was clearly infatuated by her. I was going to have to break his heart (by proxy) as well as remind him that this had breached his professional code of conduct. I decided to get it done before the patients arrived at 8.30 a.m.

Break his heart and get back to seeing patients, I said to myself as I walked down the corridor to Andy's room. *Easy*.

I knocked. 'Come in,' Andy's voice said from behind the door. He had just arrived and was unpacking his things and placing them on the desk. 'Hi Amir,' he said when he saw me.

'Hi Andy. How are you?'

'Fine,' he said as he turned on his computer. He didn't ask how I was, that wasn't Andy's style. I sat down and placed my phone on the table, opened to the screenshot of the text.

'Andy, we need to talk,' I said. He looked down, not meeting my gaze.

'I've seen the text, Andy,' I said.

'Where?' he asked quietly, still looking down.

'Charlotte came to see me this morning.'

Silence.

'Andy, did you send this text?'

'Yes,' he said.

Andy was starting to flush. He did this when he felt uncomfortable; it would begin with red blotches on his neck that would slowly engulf his face. I felt sorry for him, but I had to press on. Break his heart and get back to seeing patients.

'Andy, I have to say, this is not appropriate behaviour for the workplace,' I said. 'Do you understand that?'

Andy didn't say anything.

'Charlotte is quite upset by this. She came to see me this morning and is keen to nip this in the bud,' I continued. I was finding it difficult to find the correct tone for this conversation as Andy wasn't giving me anything back.

I left a silence, hoping that Andy would sense he would have to fill it.

'But she feels the same,' he said quietly.

'No, Andy, she doesn't. She is happily engaged; all she talks about is her wedding. She really doesn't feel the same. I'm sorry.' I was trying to find a balance between being honest with him and being supportive.

'She does, I've spoken to her, she feels the same,' Andy said, his voice rising now.

'Andy, she described that as banter, it wasn't anything romantic. She told me today she wants to put an end to this.' I had to try the direct approach; it was coming up to half past eight. The patients would be arriving soon and expecting to be seen. I had to get this message across to him.

Andy stiffened. 'If that's what she said to you then that's it then. Tell her I won't bother her again.'

'Andy, you still have to maintain a professional relationship with her. But I think it's best if you try to minimise your interaction with her. There are other nurses you can go to if you need to,' I said.

'Yes, I will do that,' Andy said slowly.

'Okay, well that's settled then. I'll tell Charlotte I have spoken with you,' I said. Andy nodded.

I left the room feeling rather proud of myself. I had handled that well. *Very professional*, I thought.

An hour later, I got a message from our reception manager. Andy had gone home with a migraine and she wanted to know what to do with his patients.

'I'll see them,' I messaged her back grimly. Perhaps I hadn't handled it as well as I had thought.

Andy didn't come back to work the rest of that week. It was clearly a mother of a migraine. I felt a little responsible for Andy not coming back, so I sent him a text to make sure he was okay but got no response. This wasn't like him; Andy was the type of person to respond to messages and emails immediately. Sometimes I wondered if he just sat there waiting for messages to arrive so he could reply.

Word had already got out about me almost killing a medical student with the use of cats. I didn't also want to be the GP trainer known for derailing a GP trainee's career!

I decided to ring him on Saturday morning. The phone rang for some time before he answered. I was expecting it to go to voicemail, so his 'hello?' caught me off guard.

'Hi Andy, it's Amir,' I said, immediately feeling silly. Of course he would know it was me, he had my number stored on his phone. 'I'm just ringing to see how you are.'

'I'm feeling much better, thank you.' His reply was curt.

'It's just that we haven't heard anything from you this week, and we weren't sure if you would be returning to work.'

'I am going to see how I feel on Monday and decide whether I can come in or not,' he said, his voice sounding colder than usual.

I was getting a bit fed up. I understood it would be difficult for Andy to face Charlotte, but he was supposed to be an almost fully qualified GP and he was behaving like a jilted teenager. Although I am sympathetic to people who cannot come to work for health reasons, if truth be told it is a royal pain in the neck when clinicians ring in sick. Patients tend to be booked in well in advance, and often these patients have planned these appointments carefully and scheduled their entire day around them. It was time Andy came back to work.

'Andy, I am going past your house later today,' I lied. 'Why don't I pop in for a cup of tea?'

Now it was Andy's turn to be caught off guard. He couldn't very well tell me he was going out if he was too unwell to come to work. 'Oh, um, well okay, if you're passing by.'

'Great, see you in about half an hour.' I hung up before he had a chance to come up with an excuse.

Andy lived alone. He opened the front door as I pulled into his drive, wearing a smart shirt and trousers which I thought was a bit odd for a weekend. He led me through the hallway and into the living room. Andy had told me not long after starting with us that he was an only child. His dad had been an accountant and his mum a teacher. His dad had died when Andy was at medical school, during his final year. His mum hadn't told him at the time as he was sitting his final-year exams and she didn't want it to derail them as he had worked so hard. As a result, Andy had missed his own father's funeral. When most other medical students were celebrating the end of five years at university, Andy was mourning the loss of his father. This had been the only time I had seen Andy show any real emotion. Sadly, two years later, Andy's mum had also died.

There was a small cabinet in the hallway, which had pictures of both his parents on. I stopped to look at them, as Andy carried on into the living room.

'Shall I take your jacket?' Andy asked.

'No, it's okay. I'll keep hold it for now.' It was cold and I wasn't about to give up my coat just yet. Andy read my thoughts.

'Sorry, it's just me here so I hardly ever turn on the heating. I don't often get visitors,' he said.

'I am sorry for just turning up,' I said, trying not to look cold. 'I just wanted to make sure you were okay after what happened last week. I know it wasn't easy for you.' I stopped short of saying it wasn't easy for me either. I had to tread carefully.

Chapter 8

'I am, thanks. I had a migraine – I get them from time to time and I just felt it best if I rested until it subsided.'

'Of course, I understand.' I looked around the room. 'Is that your dad with Margaret Thatcher?' I said, pointing at a photograph that took centre stage on the mantelpiece.

'Yes, he had very different political views to me. We used to argue about it all the time,' Andy said with a hint of a smile. I nodded.

'Is it tea you drink?' he said, getting up.

'Yes please, just milk. Can I use your bathroom?' The cold had made my bladder constrict and now I was desperate for a pee. Andy gestured upstairs.

The bathroom was spotless but in need of an update. I made my way back down the corridor and noticed a door with the words 'Andy's Room' on it. The sign looked like it had been made years ago and the letters were all in different colours. It was the kind of sign you would expect to find on the door of a child's bedroom. I paused for a minute until I was sure I heard the clink of cups in the kitchen and then poked my head around the door.

I knew I shouldn't have done it, but curiosity got the better of me. If this had been a horror movie, I would have come to a sticky but brutal end, and I daresay I would have deserved it. But instead I felt I had been transported back in time. The room was that of the teenage Andy; there was a mobile solar system suspended from the ceiling and pictures of animals on the wall. There was a fully constructed Tyrannosaurus rex standing on the corner of the desk, next to Andy's stethoscope and GP books. The bed hadn't been made up since the morning and net curtains made it feel a bit dingy.

Andy was waiting for me downstairs with a very weak-looking cup of tea and an unopened packet of ginger biscuits.

'I didn't know if you wanted biscuits?' Andy said.

'Just the tea, thanks,' I said taking a large lug.

'Andy, do you mind me asking if you were close to you father?' Sometimes, even on your days off, you can't help but treat some conversations as a consultation, and clearly Andy had some unresolved issues with his parents.

Andy looked taken aback by the question. 'Yes, we were very close,' he said in a way that meant he didn't want me to ask anything else. I took the hint.

We talked about a difficult patient I had seen and I asked Andy what he would have done in the same situation. It was nice to get back on to familiar territory with him. We didn't talk about his parents again, nor did I mention I had been a terrible house guest and had taken it upon myself to look in his room.

But I was glad I had come, I felt I now understood Andy's reasons for being more reserved than my other trainees. I thanked him for the cup of tea.

'You know, Andy, we would all like it if you came back to work on Monday,' I said, without pressing the point too hard.

'Yes, I think I will probably be feeling better by then,' he said.

Andy didn't wait for me to get into the car before closing the door. He was going to have to brush up on his manners if he had any hope of finding a girlfriend!

When Andy came back, things settled down between him and Charlotte and I heard he went on to have a very successful GP career elsewhere. But I often wondered whether he ever did find himself a partner and if he had managed to escape the stifling confines of his childhood home. If ever there was a fledgling that needed to leave the nest, it was him.

Every August, the old trainees leave and a new eager batch arrive. An eager new set of faces who are keen to get involved and show us what they have got. When new trainees begin with us at our surgery, they have a two-week induction programme. This involves them sitting in with myself and the other doctors watching us consult. It also gives us some time to get to know them.

This year my trainee was called Dr Angela Monarch. She was from Harrogate, a beautiful town in North Yorkshire with quaint shops, spas and tea rooms aplenty. It's where you go when you want to show people the nice parts of Yorkshire – the kind of place you would take your mother for Mother's Day. Where I live now is very different. It is charming in its own way, but it's never going to be overrun with mums on scenic day trips.

Angela was sitting in with me. I was on call. People often ask me what it means when a GP is on call. Most people understand the concept of a hospital doctor being on call for emergencies – if nothing else they have seen it on TV. The doctor's phone goes off and there is a dramatic emergency that they have to rush in for, usually involving a six-car pile-up, severed limbs and then life-saving surgery in a darkened theatre room. Well, it's not quite as dramatic when a GP is on call.

Basically, after all the appointments have been given out in the morning (which is minutes after the phone lines open), any additional patients who feel their medical problem needs to be dealt with that day go on a telephone list for me and I assess whether or not it is a true emergency.

On this particular day I had a call from a nursing home. One of our elderly patients had been taken ill during the night and they felt she was struggling to breathe. I told them I would come out and visit her.

'Come on, Angela, let's go,' I said, putting on my coat and packing my bag. 'We have a 79-year-old lady who sounds like she might have pneumonia. I'll drive.'

Angela put on her coat and followed me out to the car park. We got into the car and made our way to the nursing home. After parking up, we pressed the buzzer to be let inside. No answer. We pressed again. No answer.

'I'll just phone them,' I said, overly cheerful for Angela's benefit. I punched in the number and let it ring. We waited for a few minutes before someone answered.

'Hello?' a harassed voice said.

'Hi, it's Dr Khan, I am here to see Mrs Higgins. I'm standing outside and nobody is answering the door.'

'Sorry, all the staff are busy. I'll be right there,' the voice said.

Moments later, a nurse came to the door. She looked tired; her hair was tied up in a bun but there were loose strands escaping at all angles, giving her a slightly wild look. Her name badge said Elspeth Moore.

'Come in, Dr Khan. Sorry, I have had staff off sick today, so it's been busy.'

'Don't worry, I understand,' I said. 'This is Angela; she is one of our GP trainees.'

'Hello,' Angela said. Elspeth smiled at her.

'I'll just go and get Mrs Higgins' notes,' Elspeth said as she went into her office. We were left standing in the corridor. It was slightly depressing. There was the faint smell of urine in the air and the wall was adorned with photographs of the residents that lived in the home. Most of the photos had been taken at a party of some sort, so the scenes showed a collection of elderly people forced to wear paper party hats and look at the camera while a grinning carer linked arms with them.

I moved away from the photo wall and looked at the 'activities' board. There was long list of potential activities that were supposedly offered each day for the residents. The list included ballroom dancing and board games. Next to the list was a white board which displayed '*Today's Activity*'. On it was scrawled with green marker pen: '*Watching TV*'.

Funny, I thought, *watching TV certainly isn't on the list of potential activities advertised*. I remembered that poor Elspeth was short-staffed and let the thought go.

Elspeth appeared again, carrying a large folder.

'Maureen Higgins is on the third floor,' Elspeth said, walking past us and motioning for us to follow. 'She was fine yesterday, though the night staff reported she didn't eat all of her dinner. During the night they noticed she was coughing more and struggling with her breath. They did give her some of her inhaler which settled it down for a while, but she is still very drowsy and more confused than normal.'

'Has she managed to get out of bed today?' I asked.

'No, she didn't want to.'

'Has she had anything to drink today?'

'She is only having sips, not much, and she hasn't passed urine today. That's what got us worried.'

Elspeth was right to worry – the fact that an elderly lady was not drinking and not passing urine suggested a serious infection. Elderly people are prone to infections spreading rapidly through their bodies and causing acute kidney failure. I explained all of this to Angela as we climbed the stairs and she nodded solemnly.

We entered Mrs Higgins' bedroom. It was pristine. There was a neat dressing table with a selection of hairbrushes on it and a chair that faced out to the window and on to the car park. On the wall was a photo of Maureen Higgins on her wedding day, sitting on a wall in front of the church, her new husband sitting next to her with his arm around her, pulling her into him. Although the photograph was in black and white, it had clearly been a beautiful day as there was not a single cloud in the sky. Surrounding the wedding photo was a selection of other wedding and graduation photos depicting Maureen's family, all displayed proudly above the bed she now lay in.

Maureen was propped up in bed. Her hair, which I imagine she once took great pride in given the number of hairbrushes on display, was flattened against her head and she had her eyes closed.

'Maureen, the doctor is here to see you.' Elspeth placed her hand gently on Maureen's arm and gave it a shake. Maureen opened her eyes and made a grunting sound.

'Hello Mrs Higgins,' I said. 'My name is Dr Khan and I have Dr Monarch with me. We have come to see you as we heard you weren't feeling too well.'

Maureen grunted again, her eyes closed again. She tried to prop herself further up the bed, realised she didn't have the energy and gave up.

'It's okay, Mrs Higgins, don't try to get up, I can assess you where you are.' She looked exceptionally small underneath the sheets. Her legs were bent at the knees and tucked underneath her, making her look even smaller. Her cheeks were sunken and a myriad of lines ran across her face. Her hands hung loosely together under her chest; someone had painted her fingernails a pale pearly pink but the colour was at odds with the green veins that criss-crossed the back of her hands. She didn't have her false teeth in so her lips curled inwards as her mouth was slightly parted, revealing a pale pink palate.

I started to unpack my bag. Her breathing was laboured; I could see the rise and fall of her chest. With every exhale there was a grunt, signalling the effort it was taking Mrs Higgins to simply take air in and out.

Chapter 8

I checked her temperature, measured her respiratory rate and blood pressure and finally I listened to her chest. When a doctor listens to a chest, they are listening for the smooth sound of air moving in and out of the lungs' tunnels. Sometimes if there is fluid on the lungs from infection or pooling from the heart we hear crackles as the air moves through the fluid. In Mrs Higgins' right lung I heard nothing. There was no air movement. I was worried she had an infection so severe the fluid had engulfed the airways completely. It would explain her symptoms.

'I think she has a severe pneumonia,' I said to Elspeth. 'Angela, have a listen to her chest and tell me what you think.' It would be good experience for Angela, but more importantly, I wanted a second opinion on what I had just heard. Angela whipped out her stethoscope and listened in, moving from the right lung to the left, back to the right again, listening intently.

'I can't hear much on the right side,' she said timidly.

'No, neither could I.' I turned to Elspeth. 'I think we should call for an ambulance, she is very unwell and needs to be in hospital.' Elspeth nodded and looked at me expectantly. 'I will call them then,' I said, pulling out my phone from my pocket. I dialled for an emergency ambulance, explaining the seriousness of the situation and was told a blue-light ambulance would be dispatched.

I turned back to my patient. 'Mrs Higgins, I am very worried about your chest, I think you may have a serious infection and need to go to hospital.' Mrs Higgins opened her eyes and grunted. I knew that look, I had seen it before. Elderly people worry about going into hospital and never coming out. She was right to be concerned. Sometimes whatever they went in with didn't improve and killed them. And not only that, but sometimes they picked up something new in hospital, something that they would never have got if they had stayed at home, and it was that which ended up killing them.

'I know it's worrying, Mrs Higgins,' I said, gently rubbing her arm, 'but it's not the kind of infection that can be treated with tablets. I think you really need strong antibiotics through a drip.' She grunted and closed her eyes again. I took that to mean she had consented.

'I'll ring her family,' Elspeth said.

The ambulance would take some time and I was still on call back at the surgery. I imagined the ever-growing list of patients who needed to be seen that day was growing longer and longer. But I couldn't leave Mrs Higgins until I knew the ambulance was there. I turned to Angela.

'If a patient is stable we can go back to the surgery, but as Mrs Higgins is so unwell I think it's best we stay here until the ambulance arrives,' I said. 'We also need to write a letter for the hospital, detailing our findings.' Angela nodded.

I sat down at the dressing table and began writing. Then, glancing up out of the window, I saw the ambulance approaching in the distance.

'They're here,' I said to Angela. 'Let's go downstairs and hand over in the car park, that way we can get back to the surgery quicker.'

Angela and I grabbed our bags, said goodbye to Mrs Higgins and headed out to the car park. The ambulance turned into the road the nursing home was on. Except it wasn't an ambulance that I had seen, it was an ice-cream van. A bright yellow ice-cream van with the words '*Mr Whippy*' emblazoned on the top of it. As it turned into the road it switched on a familiar jingle – an instrumental version of the 'Macarena' – signalling to all the children in the street it had arrived. It played until the van parked up, a few yards from the nursing home.

Chapter 8

I looked at Angela, who clearly understood I had mistaken an ice-cream van for an ambulance. I should have been embarrassed; I should have looked sheepish and made up a reason for dragging her outside unnecessarily. But all I could think of was that I hadn't had time for lunch earlier and that I was famished.

I could see the pictures of ice creams stuck to the glass of the van.

'Do you fancy a 99?' I asked.

'Erm, I'm good, thank you,' Angela said politely.

'Okay, well I think I'm going to get one.' I walked over to the Mr Whippy and joined the queue of people that had materialised. I returned with a double-coned 99, complete with two flakes. It was delicious. If I was going to sit outside waiting for an ambulance, I might as well be eating an ice cream, I thought.

I was pulled out of my ice-cream daze by the sound of sirens getting progressively louder. The ambulance had arrived. I tried hopelessly to guzzle down my ice cream before they arrived. It was too late, the ambulance pulled into the car park and two female crew members got out.

They took their emergency bags out of the back and started towards the front door of the nursing home.

'Angela, do you have a napkin?' I asked, hoping to wipe away the ice cream I could feel around my mouth.

'No, sorry,' Angela said. She was looking even more embarrassed than me.

Great, I thought. I wiped my mouth with the back of my sleeve and looked around for a bin to put the rest of my ice cream in. Why on earth had I ordered a double 99? There was no bin.

The ambulance crew walked past us to the door.

'Oh hello, I am Dr Khan. I called the ambulance for the patient,' I called out to them.

They stopped and looked at me, then at the ice cream which was now starting to melt and drip down the back of my hand. I gave the side that was melting a lick.

'You're the doctor?' the dark-haired one asked.

'Yes,' I said, looking back at my ice cream and giving it another lick. 'Sorry, I haven't had any lunch and the ice cream was just there.' They didn't look impressed.

'Is the patient inside?' she asked, ignoring my explanation.

'Yes, she is a 79-year-old lady who has been unwell for 24 hours. I suspect she has a right-sided pneumonia.' I licked my ice cream again. 'Possibly an empyema, very poor air entry on the right.' Another lick.

The light-haired ambulance crew member was looking at me in utter disbelief.

'Here is the letter,' I said, handing it over to them. To my horror, some of the strawberry sauce from my ice cream had somehow found its way onto the letter, leaving a sticky red trail on the text. I ignored it.

The dark-haired crew member looked at the letter, opened up her emergency bag and pulled out a pair of latex gloves. She slowly and deliberately put on the gloves and took the letter from me. *There's no need for that*, I thought.

'Thank you, doctor. We will take it from here.' She turned on her heels and headed back towards the door. The lighter-haired one stared at me for a moment longer, gave a faint shake of her head and followed her colleague.

'Right,' I said to Angela. 'Best get back to work, I imagine we will have lots to do when we get back.' I wolfed down the ice cream in the car and left a sticky set of hand prints on the steering wheel as I drove us back to the surgery. Angela looked mildly horrified by my behaviour. I expect the good doctors of

Chapter 8

Harrogate didn't smother themselves in strawberry sauce when their patients were gravely ill.

Mrs Higgins spent eleven days in hospital before succumbing to her infection. The cause of death stated on her death certificate was sepsis secondary to pneumonia. Sadly, the infection had caused her kidneys to fail and that eventually led to her demise.

You do have those moments where you wonder whether sending elderly people into hospital is really what's best for them. I have seen elderly couples say tearful goodbyes to each other when one of them is admitted to hospital. There is an unspoken understanding between people of a certain age that hospitals may no longer mean what they once did – a place to be treated for illness and to convalesce. They are now considered dangerous places, a preamble to your final resting place where you aren't able to wear your own clothes or be among the familiarity of your own belongings. Where family members are only able to visit in pairs and you are surrounding by beds that are filled by people who are on the same journey as you, some of whom have a one-way ticket only.

As a GP you are stuck. Do you leave them at home, knowing they are unlikely to make it through the weekend? Or do you take your chances at the hospital? It is something that all our trainees will have to learn to decide for themselves once they become a fully qualified doctor – and it is my job to teach them the decision-making process. I hope that Angela had learned something from her trip to see Mrs Higgins – even if it was only how *not* to make a good impression with a visiting ambulance crew.

Chapter Nine

I was feeling rather proud of myself. I had arrived especially early to work that morning to get ahead of things. I had filed my blood results, composed my hospital letters, completed my insurance reports, written several referral letters and read my GP trainee's learning log entries on their portfolio. It was not even 8 a.m. and I was feeling very smug.

I drank my coffee, wondering what I might do in the next fifteen minutes before my patients came in. A spare fifteen minutes, what a luxury! I lay back in my chair, thinking I would just do nothing.

My moment of serenity came to an abrupt end when I heard a frantic knock on the door. Gerard, our caretaker, burst into the room.

'Amir, a patient is fitting in the queue in reception. There aren't any other doctors around,' he said urgently. I grabbed my unpacked bag and ran.

I could see two of our receptionists crouching down beside a patient who was having a seizure. It was a young lady, no more than twenty-five years old. Her eye were closed, teeth clenched and her rigid limbs were pushed out straight. She was making guttural sounds.

'Get the crash trolley,' I said to Gerard, 'and see if any of the nurses are around.'

Chapter 9

'We've called for an ambulance,' Bronwyn, one of the receptionists, told me. 'She was standing in line, waiting to be booked in, then made a strange noise before falling to the floor. She has been fitting for about two minutes.'

Although as a doctor you are trained to deal with most emergencies, it is always a bit bewildering when the emergency is in full view of the public. I could see the other patients who had been waiting for an appointment staring at me.

Gerard arrived with the crash trolley. I moved quickly, turning her on her side, checking her blood sugar and pulse. She had been fitting now for over three minutes and we needed to give her something.

'Gerard, please get the mobile curtains.' Gerard disappeared again. The mobile curtains were a set of privacy curtains on wheels. We had had people collapse in the waiting room before and even though they may not have been conscious, they were still entitled to some privacy. Gerard wrapped the curtains around the patient, shielding her from the stares.

The patient was showing no signs of coming out her seizure. She was entering the realms of prolonged seizure activity or status epilepticus, which is a medical emergency that carries a 20 per cent risk of death.

Rupal, one of nurse practitioners, arrived.

'Rupal,' I said, speaking quickly, 'can you check this lady's records to see if she has a history of epilepsy?'

'Yes,' Rupal replied. 'I saw her last week; she definitely has epilepsy.'

That was all I needed to know. I got the vial of midazolam out of the crash trolley and squeezed the contents into the patient's mouth. Midazolam is a powerful sedative and relaxant.

It did its job: the patient started to relax, the noises stopped and her body became less rigid.

I breathed a sigh of relief and put an oxygen mask around her face.

I checked her pulse and blood pressure one more time, then had to stand up, as my legs were cramping from all the crouching down. The patient was beginning to regain consciousness and was pulling at her face mask. I explained to her what had happened and she told me her name was Donna.

The ambulance arrived and Donna managed to get up and sit in their wheelchair, ready to be taken to hospital for further tests.

'No, no, I can't go yet!' Donna cried as the paramedics started wheeling her out. 'My handbag, I had a handbag with me when I came in.'

We all scanned the floor for a handbag. None of us could see anything.

'Are you sure you had it with you?' I asked Donna. It wasn't unusual for people who had come out of seizures to be a bit confused.

'Yes, it's a brown leather one, it's got my phone and house keys in. I remember taking it out with me this morning.'

We searched again and Gerard made an announcement in the waiting room to see if anyone had seen it. Nobody replied.

'I am not leaving without it,' Donna said. She was getting tearful. Poor thing, it had been a bad start to the day for her.

Gerard made another announcement. 'There is CCTV in this waiting room, so if anybody has taken this young girl's handbag they'd better speak up now,' he said firmly. 'Otherwise, I will take a look at the footage and will be calling the police.'

Chapter 9

The people in the waiting room looked at each other; some were shaking their heads or making vague attempts to look under their seats to check it wasn't there.

'Mum,' a child's voice said, 'isn't that it there?' The child pointed to a brown bag that had been stuffed between the child and his mother.

The mother stared at her child and then looked at me and Gerard.

'Oh yes, there it is,' she said. 'I picked it up to keep it safe. Thanks for reminding me.' She handed it over to Gerard, looking sheepish. Gerard gave her a look, took the bag and placed it on Donna's lap.

Gerard looked at me. 'You wouldn't believe some of the stuff that goes on in this waiting room,' he said, loud enough for the lady who took the handbag to hear. We took the crash trolley back to the nurse's room. It wasn't even 8.30 a.m.

I returned to my room and winced as I took a sip from my coffee, which had now gone cold. Putting it to one side, I called in the first patient, Hanna Kovacs.

Scanning her records, I could see she was a Hungarian national who had only registered with us a few months ago. She had only been to see us once before, when she had an early pregnancy miscarriage. The appointment note said she wanted to talk about something 'personal'.

When patients make appointments to see a doctor, receptionists are trained to ask them to give a brief description of the problem. This is not because the receptionist is being nosey in any way, in fact most would rather not ask, but modern general practice has changed so much these days that in any one surgery you are likely to find a mix of GPs, advance practitioners, physiotherapists, pharmacists and mental health workers. This means the reception staff, using a carefully designed navigation system, can direct patients to the most appropriate clinician. I think this idea is going to take some time for the general public to accept, as most people seem stuck on the old idea of a doctor being the right person for all things medical.

'Come in,' I said as Hanna knocked on the door. 'Hi, Hanna, my name is Dr Khan.' I smiled as she came in, accompanied by an older Indian man. He looked familiar, but I couldn't quite place him. 'How can I help?'

Neither of them said anything. Hanna looked at the floor and the Indian man looked at her, willing her to say something.

'Hanna, would it be easier if we talked alone?' I asked.

She shook her head nervously.

'Okay, well anything you say to me will be kept in the strictest of confidence, so you needn't worry about anything,' I said softly.

She still didn't look up.

'Shall I tell Dr Khan what's been happening?' the Indian man said. Hanna shrugged.

I preferred patients to speak for themselves, especially when it wasn't clear what the relationship between people in the room was. But it seemed this was the only way I was going to get any information.

'I'm Mr Patel, Hanna's neighbour.' Now I recognised him – Mr Pritpal Patel was one of our patients. Mr Patel looked at Hanna for confirmation and she gave a faint nod. 'You see, Hanna didn't want to come today, it has taken me a long time to get her here.'

I didn't say anything. I didn't want to interrupt the flow of conversation; clearly something very sensitive was going on.

Chapter 9

'Hanna moved in next door six months ago, with her boyfriend,' Mr Patel continued. 'It hasn't been a good relationship. My wife and I can hear them arguing next door. It happens very late at night when her boyfriend gets back from work.'

Mr Patel paused, looking at me and then at Hanna. 'My wife told me not to interfere, that it was a private matter between two people, but we could hear the fights and the noises coming through the walls. I couldn't leave it.'

I put down the pen I had a habit of fiddling with when talking to patients and leaned forward.

'Hanna, do you want to tell me about these arguments with your boyfriend?' I asked. She shrugged again. 'Can they get violent?' She nodded. 'Hanna, are there any children at home with you?' She shook her head, violently.

'I waited until her boyfriend went to work before going around,' Mr Patel continued. 'The night before there had been a fight. Hanna didn't want to tell me anything at first. He has taken away her phone and she doesn't have any family or friends here. She doesn't have any money either, except for what he gives her.'

'Is that correct, Hanna?' I asked, and she nodded again.

'Last week, I bought her a pay-as-you-go phone so she could call her family in Hungary,' Mr Patel said. 'Or me if she needed me.'

I looked at Mr Patel, who must have been in his late seventies. I was taken aback by his kindness. He must have read my mind.

'I am an old man, Dr Khan. It takes a lot to frighten me.'

'I think you are more than just an old man, Mr Patel. I think you are a very brave man and Hanna is lucky to have you as her neighbour.' I turned to Hanna. 'Hanna, I know this is very difficult, and you have to be brave too. What your boyfriend is doing to you is not right, you do not deserve this. Has he left any marks on you?'

She looked at Mr Patel who nodded, then lifted up her blouse. A deep purple bruise marked her right flank, and another bruise was partially visible just above it. I went to touch the bruise but Hanna immediately lowered her blouse.

'Sorry, Hanna, I was just seeing if it was still tender.' I pushed my chair back, creating a safe distance between us. I needed her to feel comfortable. 'Hanna, what he is doing to you is a criminal offence. There are organisations I can call for you who will help you find a safe place to stay. Would you like me to call them? You wouldn't have to go home today.'

Hanna looked up at me. There was very little emotion in her eyes.

'I can't leave,' she whispered in a thick Hungarian accent. 'I can't.'

'I know it will be difficult, Hanna, but it is the right thing to do,' I said.

'I have no family here, no friends.' She looked scared now. 'No money.'

'These organisations will help you, and they will keep you safe,' Mr Patel said. 'This is what we talked about.'

Hanna shook her head. 'I am sorry, I can't.' She was sobbing now. 'He will find me.'

'Hanna, we can speak with the police. They will make sure he won't come after you, you can even press charges if you want to,' I said.

Adult domestic violence cases were difficult. I had a young lady in front of me whose partner had beaten her black and blue and she was talking about going back to him, but there was

Chapter 9

nothing I could do without her consent. There were no children or third parties at risk, so my hands were tied. I couldn't go against her wishes.

'Hanna, you do know that it won't get better? That one day he might hurt in a way that you may not recover from?' I had to make sure she understood the risks.

'Hanna, please let Dr Khan help,' Mr Patel said.

Hanna looked at me and then at Mr Patel. 'You know, my father used to beat my mother. He would do it in front of me and my sister, and we would run upstairs. I would be so scared I would wet myself.' She paused. 'One time, we were both hiding in our room, and a monster came through the door. The monster had a red face and big fat lips and it knew we were in there. It came through the door and locked it behind it. It was worse than the monsters you see in these films or read about in books. It came straight for us. My sister was quiet but I was crying loudly. I closed my eyes as tight as I could. I thought the monster was going to eat us both. But it didn't, it put its finger against my lips to quieten me.' Tears streamed down Hanna's face.

'The monster was scared too. It was hiding from something. When I opened my eyes, the monster was close enough for me to see who it was. It was my mother. Her face had been beaten by my father; it was red with blood and her lips and eyes were swollen. I was five years old.'

'Hanna, this is why you must leave him. You have seen what can happen if you stay,' I pleaded with her. I was hoping her telling me this story was the beginning of her seeing that staying would be wrong.

'I can't leave, doctor,' she said. 'This is my life now, to be just like my mum.'

I wasn't having this. 'Can you not see that if you stay and you have children with him, you will be putting your children in exactly the same situation you were in?'

'Maybe he will change when we have children,' Hanna replied.

'He won't,' I said.

Hanna wiped her face with her hands, and got up. 'I am sorry for wasting your time, doctor.' She looked at Mr Patel. 'And yours, Mr Patel.'

Mr Patel stood up too. 'Please don't go back there,' he begged.

'I want to go home now,' Hanna said flatly.

'Hanna, if you ever change your mind, here is card with a number you can call. These people will help you.' I handed her one of our domestic abuse cards. 'Or you can come straight to the surgery and we will help.' She took the card and put it into her pocket. Mr Patel looked at me apologetically and gave a slight shake of his head before walking out with her.

I took a deep breath. I was upset about Hanna, but I was mostly angry. Angry that her boyfriend could get away this, angry that Hanna wouldn't leave him, but mostly angry that I was powerless to help. Confidentiality overruled everything in this case, and if Hanna didn't want me to inform the police, there was nothing I could do about it.

I typed up my notes, paying particular attention to describing the bruises accurately. You never knew when such information would be needed.

I was running twenty minutes behind now. My appointments are booked at ten-minute intervals with no time added to write detailed notes. Most patients accepted that GPs sometimes ran behind; they knew this meant the doctor was

Chapter 9

dealing with complex patients that required more than the allocated ten minutes. They also knew that if their problem needed more than ten minutes, they would get it. There was the odd person who complained about the wait, but most were understanding.

Emily Ashworth had been booked in to see me next. She had had her surgery but unfortunately there had been some complications. The surgeons had inspected her heart and replaced the old shunt with a new one. Emily had been taken to the intensive care unit after her surgery, still intubated and under the effects of the anaesthetic. Her oxygen levels had dipped worrying low, so a decision was made to keep her breathing tube in for longer than initially anticipated. Three days after the procedure they attempted to wake her up and take her tube out, but unfortunately she struggled to breathe on her own. After her oxygen count dropped to life-threatening levels, she was immediately sedated and tubed again.

I had spoken with her mum, Wendy, about it at the time. She was fraught with anxiety. She spent every night at the hospital, her other daughters staying at their grandfather's.

When they tried to take the tube out for the second time, it was found that Emily's vocal cords had become paralysed, most probably as a result of having repeated tubes down her throat over the years. The team at the hospital were left with no option but to put a tracheostomy tube in Emily's throat to help her breathe on her own. This involved making an incision in her throat, below the paralysed vocal cords, and putting in a small plastic tube which was inserted to keep it open and to allow air in and out.

It's a bad enough procedure for an adult but it was highly traumatic for Emily who was only five.

Emily wasn't talking when she came to see me. She didn't bring a stuffed toy with her this time. She didn't want to sit alone in the chair so Wendy kept her on her lap.

'I think she has an infection in her tracheostomy site,' Wendy said. She looked like she hadn't slept for weeks. Her eyes were dull and her cheeks sunken. 'There is a lot of green phlegm coming out of it.'

It was the first time I had seen Emily since her operation and I could see the tube in her throat and a bandage wrapped around her neck keeping it in place. The bandage was soggy from saliva and phlegm at the site of the tracheostomy.

'How is she coping with it?' I said.

'Badly. We have to take the tube out every so often to clean it and then re-insert it. They've taught me how to do it at the hospital but she hates it. She gets very distressed, which of course makes her go blue and then I panic. I have asked the nurses to come out and do it, but even they struggle with her.'

I could only imagine what Emily and Wendy must have been going through.

Emily backed away as I tried to examine the tracheostomy site.

'It's okay, darling, I'm just going to take a look,' I said as I moved in slowly. Her breathing became more rapid and she twisted away from me.

'Dr Khan just wants to take a look, Emily,' Wendy said.

The skin around the tube was inflamed and sore-looking. It was no wonder Emily didn't want me to go near it.

'It is infected,' I said to Wendy. 'We will have to give her some antibiotics.'

'I thought so,' Wendy said.

Chapter 9

'Have they told you what the plan is with the tracheostomy?'

'They're going to try to take it out at the end of the month. Hopefully the vocal cords will be working by then,' Wendy said, and looked up at the ceiling in a silent prayer.

'Have they said anything about her voice coming back?'

'They just don't know. I know that that is what Emily is worried about most, her voice not coming back, isn't that right, darling? But we have been praying every night and we know only the best will happen.' She cuddled in tighter to Emily.

'Is there anything else I can do to help?' I asked, wanting to be able to take some of their worries away.

'If all goes well, the hospital has put us in touch with a charity who help children with serious illnesses, and they have said they might be able to send us all to Lapland to see Santa!' Wendy said, more to Emily than to me.

'Oh, wow, that sounds exciting!' I said.

'Yes, so Emily just has to be brave one more time. You can do that, can't you sweetie?' Wendy said. Emily nodded.

I gave them a prescription for the infection and let them go. Wendy and I both knew that Emily would have to be brave several more times after this.

The next patient was 22-year-old girl, Katie. I apologised to her for being late as she entered.

'S'alright,' she said as she sat down.

'How can I help?' I asked. The notes told me she was pregnant, but that she was still only in the first trimester.

'I had my early pregnancy scan last week,' she said. 'Have you got the results?'

I was surprised. Usually the hospital would give patients the results of obstetric scans, but they always sent us a copy for our records. I brought it up on screen.

'Yes, I have it. It says you were eleven weeks and two days pregnant at the time of the scan. Everything else looks normal,' I said, studying the scan and report.

Katie looked past me at the picture of the scan. She pulled out her paper copy from her handbag and placed it on the table.

'These scans, are they in colour?' she asked.

'No, they are in black and white mostly,' I replied, frowning.

'Black and white, or black or white?' She asked again.

'I don't understand your question, Katie,' I said.

'Well, can you tell if the baby is going to be black or white?'

The penny dropped. 'Oh, I see. No we can't, Katie. Not until it comes out anyway.' I looked at her expectantly. She slowly picked up her copy of the scan, folded it up and put it back in her purse. 'Is there anything else I can help with?' I asked.

She shook her head. 'No, that's all I needed to know. Thank you.' She got up and walked out.

I looked at the picture of the baby on screen. I wasn't sure how I was going to document this one, but on the plus side, the consultation had lasted five minutes so I was now only running fifteen minutes behind!

As my head hit the pillow at the end of that day, the faces of the patients I had seen earlier swam in and out of my consciousness – Donna fitting in the reception area, Hanna and Mr Patel, poor little Emily Ashworth, even Katie and her delicate situation. It had been a typically untypical day. But it was Hanna to whom my thoughts kept returning. I wondered if she was being beaten tonight, and I wondered what would happen if I just called the police. She would probably deny it to them, maybe even report me to the GMC for breaching my duty of confidentiality. No, I couldn't do it. She had to make the decision to leave; it couldn't be forced upon her by someone who she felt didn't understand her situation. I thought about Mr Patel and how he had gone to help her despite what his wife had said. I hoped I would do the same thing if I ever found myself in that situation.

As the weeks passed I thought about Hanna less and less. I would still check her notes every now and again to see if she had come back and seen someone else, but the last entry was always mine. Eventually I stopped checking them altogether.

Five months passed before I saw her again. It was after my morning clinic and I was packing my things up to go out on my visits. One of the receptionists, Tamara, came to see me.

'Amir, there is a patient at the desk asking for you,' Tamara said, looking a bit nervous.

'Do you mean she wants an appointment with me?' I asked.

'She just wants to see you – she said it was urgent and you would know what it was about.' Tamara looked at the scrap of paper she had brought in with her. 'She's a patient here, her name is Hanna Kovacs.'

I recognised the name immediately. 'Send her in, Tamara.'

Tamara showed Hanna in and left. Hanna's right eye was bruised and her top lip cut. I sat her down.

'Hanna, would you like a glass of water?' I asked her. She nodded. I left her in the room while I went to the kitchen to fetch her a drink. I was going to have to tread carefully: if I got this right, she might leave her partner today.

'What happened?' I asked, passing her the water. She took a sip.

'He found the phone,' she said. 'He found it last night and wanted to know where I got it from. He didn't believe me when I said I had bought it. He started hitting me and wouldn't stop. Normally he hits me on my body, but last night he hit my face too.' I could see talking was painful for her, as she winced with every word.

'Hanna, I am very glad you have come in to see me. What were you hoping I could do?'

'I want to leave, doctor. I want to leave; I don't want to call the police but I want to leave.'

I breathed a sigh of relief. 'Yes, of course.'

I rang the number for an organisation called Staying Put, who said they would send someone to meet Hanna at the surgery. She had left without any of her things from home, but it didn't matter, they would arrange for someone to collect them. She would be put in temporary accommodation tonight and they would take it from there. The lady who came was called Saeeda. She took Hanna, who thanked me for my help before she left.

I felt absolved. Knowing that Hanna had gone back to that home all those months ago had sat heavy with me, but now I felt lighter. I knew this was just the beginning of a very difficult journey for her, but at least she had started it.

Almost a year later, Mr Patel came to see me in clinic. I asked him if he ever heard from Hanna after she had left.

'Oh yes, she calls me often,' he said, smiling. 'She is living in London now; she works as a translator for the hospitals.'

'Oh wow,' I said. I didn't know what I was expecting. I had grown so sceptical from years of seeing people return to their abusers that I wasn't expecting a happy ending and didn't know what to do when confronted with one. 'Mr Patel, I know you don't need me to tell you this. But you were so good to support her during that time in her life.'

'I just thought that poor girl could have been my daughter, you know?' he said. 'And what if nobody helped her?' He put his hat on to go. 'I am pleased she is away from it all.'

I watched him leave, then returned to my computer. I had almost forgotten what he had come in for. Ah yes, a blood pressure review, I started documenting it.

I told the other GPs the story of how Mr Patel had helped Hanna. We agreed to send him a card with a voucher in it on behalf of the practice as well as bunch of flowers in recognition of his kindness. He tried to return the voucher to us at reception, insisting he didn't need it, but we insisted harder and he eventually took it.

Chapter Ten

People die.

You learn that fairly early on at medical school. They keep telling you to never get attached to patients or create a dependency or become too emotionally involved. It's Medicine 101. But humans are social animals, we live in social groups and we have complex social relationships. Sometimes it is impossible to turn off your emotions.

Nothing is more complex than the doctor–patient relationship. It's steeped in professionalism, confidentiality and all sorts of rules and regulations, but at the same time we encourage empathy, rapport and building a connection with a patient. It's a juxtaposition that nobody really talks about. You just have to find your own way.

I remember when I was a medical student in hospital carrying an arrest bleep. These are only given out every so often and it was the most exciting thing. For a start, they clip onto your belt and they are bright red so everybody can see you are part of the 'arrest team'. The arrest bleeps go off whenever somebody is having a cardiac arrest in the hospital, and they signify that you are now officially part of a select team that has been chosen to bring them back to life. The normal bleeps are black and a bit dowdy-looking, and have a boring, slightly irritating bleeping noise (hence the name). When the normal black bleep goes off, people just look a bit annoyed and go to the nearest phone to call the ward, only to be told there's some mundane job that has been assigned to them. When the cardiac arrest bleep goes off it sounds more like a siren. You have to drop whatever you are doing and run to the ward immediately.

I remember running through corridors packed with relatives visiting patients, one arm holding the stethoscope that I was proudly wearing around my neck and the other propelling me forward. It was very dramatic. I knew that, as a student, I would play a very small role in the attempts to resuscitate the patient but I liked the looks I got as I ran past people while the siren was going off. I imagine this is what Pamela Anderson felt like during her slow-motion running days on *Baywatch*. I felt very important.

I wasn't.

Invariably when I got there, it was a patient who I didn't know and was often old and frail-looking. There was a team of experienced people carrying out CPR. I would occasionally get the opportunity to do the chest compressions, but that was about the extent of a medical student's involvement. When they died, it was sad. But only because death is always sad, and because in the back of my mind I knew there would be some devastated relatives somewhere. But I felt detached.

It's different when you are a GP. You have looked after these people for years, you know them. You know not only about their ailments, but also about their hobbies, who their husband is, how many children they have, the fact they went on holiday to Spain last July and that you must remember to ask them about it when they next come in.

When they die, it's a bereavement.

In modern-day general practice, it's difficult for patients to see the same doctor each time they visit. Understandably, patients get fed up of telling a new doctor their story all over again from the beginning. Patients still want that idea of an old-fashioned family doctor, the type that knows all about your medical history while remembering where you like to holiday in the summer. A ten-minute consultation is usually not enough time to get to the bottom of most medical mysteries patients present with and often I will send them off for tests and investigation, and for them to come back to see another clinician for the results is frustrating. Where possible, we will try to follow up with the patients we are worried about, but if we book all of our appointments as follow-ups that leaves very little time to meet the on-the-day demand of the acutely unwell. There is just not enough give in the system and both the doctors and the patients feel it. The pressures on doctors in general practice now are such that working full time on the coal face is becoming increasingly unsustainable. Burnout among GPs is at the highest rate it has ever been, and more GPs than ever are retiring, going part time, becoming locums or taking the pressure off by varying their week with other things such as specialist clinics or education. Truth be told, this is the only way to survive general practice these days.

However, we do try our best to see the same patients when we can, and where that continuity of care is maintained the results are far superior. And sometimes that care involves helping them on their final journey.

It is not nice to think of our patients dying, but part of our job is to make sure that those who are irretrievably on that path have as comfortable a death as possible.

When I was a student a palliative care consultant told me to make sure I used the word 'dead' when talking to a family who had been bereaved.

Chapter 10

'It has finality to it,' he said. 'If you say things like "passed" or "gone" to describe a dead patient then it leaves room for ambiguity and you don't want to raise expectations.'

'Dead' felt like such a heavy-handed word, especially in such delicate situations, but years of experience have shown me he was right.

When I was a junior doctor in hospital, it was always our job to certify dead patients on the ward. We would normally get called in the middle of the night by one of the nurses to make sure a patient was dead. The nurses knew how to recognise a dead patient but the law is clear in saying that it must be a doctor who certifies a death. I would go into the room where the patient laid and there would invariably be a solitary lamp on in the corner of the room, giving things a slightly eerie feel. I would check that their pupils were not responding to my torch as well as spending time listening to their chest, checking for heart sounds and signs of breathing. By the time I had finished, the nurses would have called in any relatives and it was up to me to break the news to them, ensuring I used the word 'dead' in my explanation.

Working as a GP, we were often called to see people who had terminal illnesses and had chosen to die at home. The first time I had been called to do this was as a GP trainee. The patient was an elderly man named Mr Grayson, who was being cared for by his two sisters. He had cancer but decided he didn't want to be sent into a hospice. Nurses had been coming out to make sure he was comfortable and his two sisters, who were also elderly, had moved in with him to make sure he had the care he needed.

The sisters, Mary and Ethel, were well intentioned but out of their depth when it came to caring for him. Thankfully, this was recognised early by the hospice team and he had a pretty robust package of care for the daytime, so it was just during the night that it was left to the sisters to look after him.

I was told by the reception staff that Mary Grayson had phoned up that morning to ask if one of the doctors could come out to see her brother as he wasn't his usual self, and that this task had been assigned to me. After my morning clinic, I gathered my things and made my way over to their home.

The Graysons lived in a third-floor flat, with the sisters sharing one room and Mr Grayson in the other. There was no lift, and after Ethel buzzed me in I climbed the stairs to be greeted by the pair of them in the hallway.

'Dr Khan, thank you for coming out,' Ethel said. 'George hasn't been himself since last night. Do come in.'

'Would you like some tea?' Mary asked as she closed the door behind me.

'Thank you, that's kind but I have just had a cup,' I said. The hallway was dark and I followed them into the living room. There was the faint smell of damp in the air and the peeling wallpaper revealed blotches of mould on the exposed walls. The small window let in just enough light to illuminate a wall decorated with Catholic mementoes ranging from crucifixes to paintings of the Virgin Mary. In the centre of all the pictures was a large framed photo of the Pope.

'Please sit down.' Mary motioned me to sit on the sofa.

I moved some old newspapers out of the way and took a seat.

'Tell me, how has Mr Grayson been?' I asked them.

'We usually check him during the night,' Ethel started. 'I go in at eleven o'clock and Mary checks again about three.'

'Yes,' Mary said. 'After the nurses leave, we read him a passage from the Bible.'

Chapter 10

'It soothes him,' Ethel added.

'Yes, it soothes him. And then he likes his mouth cleaning and a sip of water before he goes to sleep.'

'Warm water, he doesn't like it cold,' Ethel said.

'Yes Ethel, the doctor doesn't need to know how warm he likes his water,' Mary said sharply. 'Last night, he didn't want any of his water. He said he wasn't thirsty.'

'Maybe it was too cold?' Ethel queried.

'Ethel, I checked the temperature and it was warm, just as he likes it.' Mary turned back to me. 'When I went to check on him again during the night, to see if he was all right, he didn't answer me.'

'And we have both been in to see him this morning and he is still sleeping, which isn't like him,' Ethel said, sounding worried. 'He is normally awake by now.'

They were staring eagerly at me. I looked at the two of them; they had clearly made an effort to get dressed in their smartest clothes. I liked that about the older generation, they still got 'dressed up' to see the doctor. The men would come to see me in clinic in a suit and tie and the women would be in smart dresses. Mary was wearing a powder-blue skirt with a white blouse, her hair had been tied up into a neat bun and she wore a crucifix around her neck. Ethel was wearing a longer black skirt with black tights and a similar white blouse, and they both sat with their hands clasped on their knees.

'Maybe I should take a look at him?' I ventured.

The curtains were still drawn in Mr Grayson's room. The only source of light was the bedside lamp. Mr Grayson was lying in bed, his head slightly turned towards the door and his mouth slack. His syringe driver stood next to him, a device designed to administer medication continuously through a small plastic tube that sat under the patient's skin. In cases where patients are in pain or distress from their illness, the medication helps lessen their symptoms.

Mr Grayson had bowel cancer. As the disease spread through his body and into his bones, it would have caused him considerable pain and the syringe driver helped keep him comfortable.

'Hello, Mr Grayson. It's Dr Khan,' I said. I am not sure why I said it. I already knew he was dead. But it seemed appropriate and the silence felt worse. 'Your sisters are worried you are still asleep so they have asked me to check in on you. I know what sisters can be like; I have six.'

It is strange being alone with a dead body. As a doctor, you are torn between being a scientist and knowing there is no feasible way they can hear you and being a human being and wanting to fill the void in the room with chatter. And who knows, maybe he could hear me?

I went through the motions of listening to his heart and checking his pupils for a reaction, but there was nothing.

I am not particularly religious, but being around a dead body has a way of finding any stray bits of faith you have hidden inside and pulling them to the forefront of your mind. And what the hell, he was clearly a religious man.

'May your soul rest in peace,' I whispered as I packed away my things.

Ethel and Mary were waiting for me outside.

'Is he going to be all right?' Mary asked.

'You know what, Mary? I will take that cup of tea please,' I said.

I made sure to say the word 'dead' in my subsequent conversation with the two sisters. In fact, I said it three times just to make sure there wasn't any confusion. Ethel kept asking if I wanted to stay for lunch, which I politely declined. I felt bad for leaving them, but the hospice nurses would be in shortly to help them with the arrangements, and I had to get back to the surgery.

As I drove back, I wondered whether Mary and Ethel would go back to their own homes now they were no longer needed to care for Mr Grayson. Caring for him had given them a renewed sense of purpose and it might be difficult for them to go back to living on their own. Death has a funny way of resetting lives and making you review your choices. I stopped at the bakery for a sandwich and bought some pastries for the staff back at the surgery. Death also has a way of making you a bit nicer for a day.

Continuity of care becomes more important when dealing with dying patients. It was important for the Graysons, and it was just as important for Mr Barrowman.

Mr Barrowman had been registered with our surgery for years. He was nearing eighty but still managed to flirt with the receptionists every time he came in. I would always know when he had come to visit as there was a monumental selection of chocolate left behind. He was secretly everyone's favourite patient.

I was particularly fond of him as we shared a passion for gardening. He had been doing it for far longer than me and would bring me in clippings from his more successful plants and an endless supply of onions over the growing season. He had a habit of downplaying any illness, which was endearing in a way, but it also meant his bladder cancer had been picked up late. He told me he had put going to the toilet more often and having the occasional blood in his urine down to 'old age', something that simply wasn't true.

Mr Barrowman was originally from Ireland and insisted everyone call him by his first name, Tom. He had been a teacher in the primary school not far from the surgery in an area where most of the houses were lived in by immigrant families.

When we finally did refer Tom to see the urologist, it was deemed too late for any active treatment to be beneficial. His cancer had spread beyond the bladder and was now in his bones. A fiercely independent man, he found it hard to admit that he could no longer come to the surgery for his appointments. He had looked particularly pale and thin when he last came in to see me.

'Tom, you know if it's too difficult for you to come here, we are more than happy to see you at home when you are not feeling well,' I had said to him.

'Blimey, I didn't think doctors did house calls any more,' he had said between breaths.

'I think I can make an exception for you,' I said.

Tom had two sons who lived in Ireland, for the last four weeks they had taken it in turns to look after him. It was one of them who had asked for us to visit that day, as he was worried that Tom's breathing had worsened and he now had a chest infection.

Tom lived on Winterbourne, one of the poorest estates in England. He had lived there before it had deteriorated into the state it was in now. These days there were old sofas tossed out onto the street and mattresses that were soaked through lying on the side of the road. There were a number of estates around where I worked, but none were quite as bad as Winterbourne. If any of our clinicians were assigned a home visit there, they were required to tell one of the managers where they were going and then report back to say they had returned safely. If they were not heard from within an hour, they would get a welfare check phone call. There was an urban legend every new doctor got told of a GP who had gone there and been stabbed and had his car stolen, though some versions involved him being mugged and beaten to a pulp, so it was hard to know what to believe. I had informed Henry, our manager, that I was going and promised I would let him know when I returned.

The estate was made up of a series of red brick semi-detached houses. It was easy to spot Tom's house, as it was the only one where the front lawn hadn't been concreted over or wasn't full of old fridges. Tom's house was pristine in comparison to the neighbouring ones; he had a perfectly manicured front lawn with rose beds either side of it. Two of the rose bushes in my own garden were grown from clippings that he had brought in for me.

Tom's son, Eamon, answered the door and took me upstairs to him. It had only been two weeks since I had last seen Tom but the difference in his appearance was stark. He had lost a lot more weight, giving his cheeks a sunken look, his eyes were only half open and his breathing was erratic and noisy.

'He started breathing like this last night,' Eamon said. 'We called the district nurses who have put something in his syringe driver to lessen his secretions, but it doesn't seem to have made much difference.'

I put my bag down and sat beside Tom. I had heard this noisy breathing before and I knew what it heralded. It was the 'death rattle', the noise a terminally ill patient makes not long before they die. As the air moves through thick secretions made up of saliva and mucus in the upper airways, it makes a characteristic rattling noise. This means the patient's internal muscles no longer have the strength to move the secretions themselves, signalling the end.

I placed my hand on Tom's.

'Hi Tom, it's Amir from the surgery, I've just been admiring your roses out front. Mine don't look as good as that, even though I have been doing everything you told me to. Are you sure you haven't been keeping something back from me?' There was no point me asking Eamon any questions about Tom's chest, it made little difference now whether he had a chest infection or not.

'Eamon, is it okay if we talk downstairs?'

I followed Eamon down to the kitchen and sat at the dining table.

'Does he need antibiotics?' Eamon asked, looking at his fingernails and trying to remove some invisible piece of dirt from them.

'Eamon, tell me what you know about how we are approaching your dad's care,' I said carefully.

He looked a bit confused. 'I know there is nothing you can do for the cancer, the consultant at the hospital told us that. But I thought there might be something you can do if he got an infection.'

'Yes, we do give antibiotics for infections if we really think they would help,' I said. This was a delicate situation. I had to make Eamon understand that the focus of Tom's care was about keeping him comfortable, keeping him out of pain, and managing the anxiety that comes with not being able to breathe properly.

'The nurses from the hospice explained why he needed the syringe driver, I understand that. And I know that we are keeping him comfortable, but surely if we can treat his chest infection that would give him a chance?' He was tearful now. 'We have to give him a chance.'

I let the silence sit in the air for a second.

Chapter 10

'Eamon, those noises you can hear when your dad is breathing aren't from an infection, they are there because he can no longer swallow his own saliva or move his own mucus.' I paused, giving him a moment to take this in. 'It won't be comfortable for him to breathe like this, so we need to increase the morphine in his driver as well as the medicine to lessen his secretions.'

Eamon didn't say anything and continued to look at his hands.

'Eamon, I don't think Tom has much time left. Do you want me to phone your brother? I think it's probably best he comes to see him now too.'

'Thank you, Dr Khan. I can phone him,' Eamon said quietly.

'I know this is difficult, but if I can just say one thing?'

Eamon stopped picking at his fingers and looked up, giving a slight nod.

'I have been looking after patients at home in their last days for many years, and I have to say the care you and your brother have provided to your dad has been exemplary. Every time I have been he has always been washed and shaved, and I know he couldn't have done those things himself. He would be proud of you both.'

'Thank you, Dr Khan. Dad wouldn't want anyone to see him without a shaven face. He made a point of having a shave every day, even on weekends.' He wiped away a tear and gave a hint of a smile.

'I'll write up his prescription before I go, and ask the district nurses to come out and administer the medication. Is there anything else I can do for you?'

Eamon shook his head. 'No, thank you for explaining it to me. I know my dad is fond of you, he told us how you shared stories of your garden when he came to see you.'

'Well, I think he was a much better gardener than me. Do you mind if I see him one more time before I go?' I asked. Eamon nodded and I made my way upstairs.

Tom was still making the death rattle noise. I didn't have anything to say to him, but I knew this was the last time I would see him. I brushed back a stray hair that had fallen onto his face. It's strange, lots of my patients have died, but this felt different. Tom had been one of those patients who I actually looked forward to seeing, as he had always had such a positive outlook on life. He had told me early on that he had taken a shining to me as I had come from a working-class background like him, and settled in the city.

'This city may not be the most glamorous place to live, Amir, but I came here, and who knows where we would have ended up had it not been for the opportunities we were given right here.'

'Goodbye, Tom,' I whispered. 'Thank you so much for the roses, I'll look after them.' I left through the front door, looking at the perfect garden one last time. I hoped whoever moved into the house next didn't pave it over like every other house on the street.

That night I went home on time to spend some time with my family, giving them an extra hug before bed.

Tom died two days later. His sons rang to thank the surgery for all we had done. An email was sent by our manager informing us of the date of his funeral, as his sons had said that anyone who wanted to come was welcome. I made a point of taking the afternoon off to attend.

Chapter Eleven

Medical professionals have to handle other people's bodily fluids on a daily basis. We have to put our fingers up bums, examine feet and genitalia. I imagine this sounds strange to people who don't work in healthcare. What is strange is that outside of work the thought of someone else's feet, urine or pus makes me feel slightly ill. But when I am at work they don't bother me. It's always a point of discussion at dinner parties – other people are constantly asking me if I ever get nauseous having to do those things and the honest answer is, no.

GPs have to do something called eight-week baby checks. This is when new parents bring in their two-month-old babies for a full top-to-toe examination to rule out any birth defects and also to give them their first immunisations. Actually, as GPs we get to do the nice bit: checking and examining the babies (which actually means fussing over how lovely they are) – and then we send them down the corridor to the nurse who takes on the 'bad cop' role of giving them their vaccinations.

Part of the eight-week baby check involves checking the baby's genitalia. There is a golden rule for examining little boys: always keep their nappies on or they will pee on your trousers. I had been carefully examining Archie who was cooing away happily on the couch. He had tried to get me with his pee but had failed miserably as I had carefully manoeuvred his nappy during the examination. I felt rather pleased with myself. It was now over and time for Archie to get dressed.

'I'll just change his nappy while he is on the couch,' Archie's mum said, producing a clean nappy from his bag.

'Here, give it me. I'll change it,' I said. Archie's mum looked tired and very comfortable sitting on the chair. I thought I would give her a longer break. She thanked me and handed me the nappy.

I pulled his old nappy out from underneath him and pulled his bottom up using his legs in order to slide in the new nappy. Archie decided to open his bowels at that point, his anus pointed directly at me. A spray of faeces left his bottom and landed on my shirt.

This was new. Nobody had warned me about this before.

Archie's mum looked horrified. 'I am so sorry. He has been a bit loose and full of wind since we changed his formula milk. The health visitor said it would settle down in the next few days.'

That story usually killed it at dinner parties.

A couple of weeks after Archie's impromptu shirt-decorating incident, my clinic was in full swing. A patient had brought me a box of chocolates earlier that morning and I had planned to put it in reception for sharing, but through the course of the clinic I had slowly made my way through all the best ones and all that were left were the Turkish delights and coffee creams. Brain food, I kept telling myself.

Clifford Barker sat down opposite me. He was a 44-year-old man with very little past medical history to speak of. It had been raining outside and his coat was wet through.

'It's rough out there,' he said.

'Looks like it – this is one the few times I'm glad to be chained to my desk,' I replied. 'How can I help, Mr Barker?'

Chapter 11

'I've had this niggling pain in my left side for the last couple of days. I just wanted to get it seen to and make sure it's nothing serious.'

'Okay, tell me about the pain itself.'

'Well, it's here on my left side.' He put his hand over his left abdomen just underneath his ribs. 'It seems to be getting worse.'

'Is it there all the time or does it come and go?'

'There is a background of pain all the time but then it gets worse in waves.'

'Anything make it better or worse?' I asked. He thought for a moment and then shook his head. I got him to lie on the couch while I had a feel of his belly. He winced slightly as I palpated the left side but it felt soft and there was nothing immediately alarming. Given Mr Barker's symptoms, I was beginning to think he may have a kidney stone.

'Mr Barker, I'd like to check your urine if that's okay, just to rule out a kidney stone. Do you think you'd be able to give me a sample?'

'Yeah, I don't see why not,' he said.

I handed him a urine pot. 'Just let me know when you are done and I will check it,' I said. We are constantly checking patients' urine, or 'liquid gold' as an old professor of mine had called it. Most clinicians use the time people take to go to the bathroom as valuable seconds to write up their symptoms. I turned back to my computer and started writing up Mr Barker's notes.

As I typed I became acutely aware that Mr Barker hadn't left the room. Instead, he pulled down his pants, took aim and started producing his sample in the pot I had given him with astonishing accuracy. He stopped just before it overflowed. He handed me the pot, still warm.

'You know, Mr Barker, most patients use the bathroom when we ask them to give us a urine sample,' I said lightly as I dipped the urine.

'I was in the Royal Marines, Dr Khan. When the doctor told you give them a sample, you dropped your pants and gave them a sample,' he said. 'Old habits and all that.'

I shrugged. I was glad that I hadn't asked for a stool sample. To be fair, he had been very time-efficient and in general practice every second counts. The dipstick showed blood in the urine which, with the pain Mr Barker was experiencing, was in keeping with kidney stones. I spoke with the urologists at the hospital who would arrange a scan and a follow-up appointment with Mr Barker.

After he'd left and I had finished writing up his notes I looked at where he had been sitting. There was a small puddle of fluid on the floor. *Oh no*, I thought. Maybe Mr Barker wasn't quite as good at controlling his bladder as I had thought. I braved a closer inspection, waiting for the smell of urine to hit me. It didn't. Thankfully Mr Barker had left only a puddle of rain water behind.

Later that afternoon, I was running our busy minor surgery clinic as usual. This was a regular clinic where patients with things like ingrowing toenails, infected cysts and troublesome lumps and bumps were referred to have them taken off. The rain had eased off by now and as my last patient for this clinic entered the room, I was already starting to think about going home and having my evening meal. It had been a long day and I was starving.

The patient was a 54-year-old man with a large infected sebaceous cyst on his back. One of my colleagues had referred him to have it removed. Mr Jones was a genial, talkative plumber whom I had met several times before, so we chatted pleasantly as he started to remove his jacket and shirt in order for me to inspect the problematic area.

Cysts are something we see commonly at the minor surgery clinic and they are always rather repulsively satisfying to remove. They are caused by a build-up of oil or pus when a sebaceous gland or its duct becomes blocked. They grow slowly and generally aren't much of a cause of concern until they become larger, at which point the pressure building up beneath the skin can become painful. In this case the cyst had also become infected, adding to the discomfort. I would need to incise the cyst to release the pus and clean out the infected area before stitching up the wound.

Once Mr Jones had removed his shirt, he lay face-down on the table so I could take a good look at it. It was as juicy a cyst as I had ever seen. Honestly, it was like a volcano ready to erupt. This was going to be fun.

I explained the procedure to Mr Jones and, with his consent, I cleaned the area, put in the local anaesthetic and got ready to make my incision. As expected, the minute I touched the cyst with my scalpel, it exploded.

Unfortunately, however, I had been concentrating hard as I performed the operation and my mouth had been slightly open. As I made the incision, some of the pus shot out and – with unerring accuracy – landed straight on my tongue.

This put me in something of a dilemma. Obviously I had to remain professional and couldn't just run away gagging, so I had to carry on with the operation and finish sewing up the wound. But I couldn't say a word with this pus still sitting on my tongue. Up till that point, Mr Jones and I had been chatting away easily as I explained what was going on and talked him through the procedure, but suddenly I was struck dumb, unable to reply to anything he asked. Understandably, he must have started to worry about my unexpected silence – had I seen something so horrifying I was unable to speak? Mr Jones tried to turn round to catch my eye and I had to use my elbow to gently pin him down and keep him still.

I don't think I have ever stitched a wound so quickly. As soon as I had put in my last stitch, I sprinted to the bathroom and washed out my mouth with soap.

'There, all done, Mr Jones! You're good to go!' I said way too heartily as I emerged from the bathroom. Mr Jones was sitting up and buttoning up his shirt, still looking a little alarmed. To make up for my earlier silence I started gabbling uncontrollably about the terrible weather we'd had that morning, which only seemed to make matters worse. Mr Jones backed out the room, staring at me strangely.

I was relieved to see him go. I needed a minute to compose myself. But somehow I had lost my appetite for my evening meal.

The next morning, the memory of Mr Jones's cyst (just about) receding, I was pleased to see who had been booked in to see me.

Emily Ashworth was talking again! She had had her tracheostomy taken out and her vocal cords had recovered. She sat opposite me, smiling.

'This is for you, Dr Khan,' she said, giving me a stuffed reindeer toy. 'It's from Santa.'

'Wooooow! Santa, really? Then I must have been a good boy,' I said, winking at her. Emily giggled.

The charity the hospital had put them in touch with had sent the entire family to Lapland last month. Wendy showed me the pictures on her phone. They had gone with other families who had sick children and Emily had made some friends.

After she had finished showing me the pictures, Wendy told me they had been assigned a children's hospice.

Chapter 11

'I always thought a hospice was where you went to die, but it isn't,' Wendy said. 'We can all go and stay over and it gives us a break from everything. There are games and activities for the kids, and I can speak with other parents about what they're going through,' she said. She looked much better today; her eyes had come back to life.

'Yes, they are really good for that kind of thing,' I said.

'Emily is fine today – we just wanted to pop in and give you your present,' Wendy said. 'We told the receptionist we didn't want to waste an appointment, but they said you wouldn't mind.'

'Of course I don't mind. You really didn't need to get me anything, but I do appreciate it, thank you,' I said. It is always a welcome surprise when a patient gets you a gift. I never expect them, but when a card or a thank-you note is put in your pigeon-hole it can make even the worst days feel better.

'Come on, Emily, we can't take up any more of Dr Khan's time,' Wendy said, pulling Emily up.

'Well, I am very glad you came, and I will have to think of a name for my reindeer,' I said to Emily.

'He has already got a name!' Emily replied.

'Has he?'

'Yes, it's Blitzen.' Then she whispered, 'Santa told me.'

'Oh, I am sorry,' I said, looking at the reindeer. 'Of course it's Blitzen!'

Emily ran over to me and hugged me. Wendy laughed. It caught me by surprise. I often hugged my older patients, especially if they were going through a particularly bad time of it, but this was a special hug. This made my day. It made all the 'icky stuff' – all the poo, wee and other bodily fluids that come my way in this job – more than worthwhile.

Chapter Twelve

It was only ten in the morning and I was tired. I could feel my eyes closing as I stared at my computer screen. The three cups of coffee I had had already felt like drops in an ocean of sleepiness.

I had been woken up at 3 a.m. that morning by a phone call from our elderly family friend, Robert. His wife, Catherine, had been short of breath for the last hour and was now experiencing chest pain.

'I didn't want to call for an ambulance if she didn't need one,' he said. 'I don't like to waste their time.'

'Robert, it really does sound like she needs an ambulance,' I had said. 'Especially if she has chest pain.'

There was a pause. I sighed.

'Would you like me to come over?' I asked.

'Only if you don't mind,' he said, sounding relieved. 'I know it's early in the morning, but I didn't know who else to call.'

'Of course, Robert, I'll be there in half an hour.' I put the phone down and got dressed. To be fair, I had told Robert and Catherine they could call me if they ever needed anything. But it had been one of those things I had said thinking they might call me to look at a sore elbow or spot on their leg and in the middle of the day.

Catherine was nearly eighty-five, and was the former head-mistress of the primary school in the centre of the village in which we had lived in. I recalled her being very excited when I had bought my first house; she had come over with a cheese and onion pie and card. We had been over to theirs for Christmas drinks and she had made one of the best Christmas cakes I had ever tasted.

Wearing my pyjamas and a duffle coat, I got into the car and drove to their home. When I rang the doorbell, Robert opened the door. He looked to have aged since the last time I saw him, but then again I imagined I looked very different to him too, having just rolled out of bed.

Catherine looked shocking. She was a proud woman who would always have a full face of make-up on whenever we saw her, so for her to let me see her like this meant she was really poorly. I already knew what I had to do before I even listened to her chest, but the two of them were hoping I would perform some miracle which meant she would not have to go to hospital. Sadly, I was not a miracle worker.

Catherine was taken off in an ambulance. I told Robert that he must come over tonight for his dinner when I returned home. It was nearly 4.30 a.m. when I got back, too late to go back to bed but too early to do anything else. I decided to go for a run to kill some time. It was a cold December morning, still pitch black, and I pounded the eerily silent streets feeling like I was the only person awake in the world.

Now I was sitting at my desk looking at my list of patients, wishing I had gone to bed when I could. To make matters worse, I was due to go on a photoshoot after my morning clinic. Well, photoshoot was a bit of a stretch, but I was supposed to have several pictures taken of me in various poses around the surgery.

It was part of a new initiative we had designed to help people with learning disabilities get used to the staff at the surgery before they came to see us. These patients found new environments and new people a challenge, so they would all get a series of photographs of the doctor and nurse they had been assigned to keep at home. The idea was that they would look at them before coming in so they would know what to expect.

It had all started the previous month when a child with a severe learning disability and behavioural issues was brought into the surgery by her parents after developing a fever and cough. The fever had come on during the night and her parents continued to give her paracetamol to keep her temperature down. They planned to get her seen first thing in the morning.

The parents drove down to the surgery at half past seven to ensure they would be first in the queue to get their daughter seen. Unfortunately, they didn't know that the demand for appointments was such that the queue can often start forming at half past six. The child was in the back of the car and, being December, it was still dark outside. Dad told Mum she should stay in the car with their daughter, Abigail, while he waited for an appointment.

When 8 a.m. came around, our appointments for that day opened up and the receptionists allocated them to people in the queue but also to those who had phoned up. By the time Abigail's father had got to the front of the line, the next available appointment was at 10.40 a.m. He was booked in to see me.

The patients had been especially complex that morning; it was the busy winter season and only minutes into the surgery opening my clinic list was full. Henry, our manager, had already been in to ask if I wouldn't mind seeing extra patients who sounded like they couldn't wait until the next day, which of course I couldn't refuse.

Chapter 12

Because of the extra patients that had been slotted in, I was running twenty minutes behind when I called Abigail in. I hadn't met her before so I briefly read through her notes first. Abigail was eight years old and had been born with a condition known as microcephaly, thought to have been caused by a virus Abigail's mum had contracted while pregnant with her. This meant she had a smaller head than expected and consequently her brain had not developed properly. She also suffered from epilepsy, which meant she had frequent seizures despite the medicine she was taking. Abigail lived with her parents and elder sister in a small house not far from the surgery. Her mum, Sarah, stayed at home full time caring for Abigail while her dad, Michael, worked as an electrician.

I called them in and waited for the knock on the door. Nothing. I pressed the icon on my computer screen to call them in again, but once again no one came. It wasn't uncommon for a patient who had been waiting to walk around to stretch their legs or take a phone call and not see the call board with their names on. I went into the waiting room.

'Abigail Lewis!' I shouted firmly. Lots of expectant faces looked at me, but nobody got up. I scanned the room but couldn't see anyone who matched Abigail's medical history. 'Annabelle,' I said, 'has my patient been here? I can't seem to find her.'

Annabelle was one of our receptionists. She had been on a pre-wedding diet a few months ago and had lost a lot of weight, but despite having been married four months now she had stuck to her diet and was very thin. She sat beside an unopened box of Celebrations chocolates a patient must have brought in. I kept a mental note of the chocolates for when I got hungry later.

165

'They went to wait in the car,' Annabelle said. 'Her dad said she was getting stressed out with all the people in the waiting room. Shall I go and get her?' I knew this was a rhetorical question; Annabelle still had a line of patient to deal with at the desk and I wasn't about to ask her to leave them to look for my patient while I just stood there.

'No, it's okay. I'll go,' I replied and headed outside. It was cold and I had no idea who I was looking for. I saw what looked to be Abigail and her family parked in one of our disabled bays. The child and her mum were in the back of the car, while Michael was sitting in the front. I knocked on the window.

'Hi, it's Dr Khan, Abigail has an appointment with me. Sorry, I have been running late,' I said as Sarah opened the door.

It looked as though Sarah had been crying. She quickly wiped her cheeks and looked up at me.

'Sorry, Dr Khan, Abigail couldn't wait in the waiting room any longer. It was too noisy for her and she doesn't do too well with unfamiliar faces.'

'That's okay,' I said. 'Shall we go inside now? We can go straight to my consulting room.'

Sarah nodded. Michael got out of the car and opened the side door where Abigail was sitting. She was strapped into a seat that had been designed especially for her.

'Darling, we are going in to see the nice doctor now,' he said softly into Abigail's ear. Abigail started screaming immediately. 'It's okay, Abigail, we'll be very quick. Dr Khan just wants to make you better.' Abigail kicked at him and started to pinch herself in protest. Sarah grabbed at her hands so she couldn't hurt herself any more.

I made a quick decision.

Chapter 12

'Would it be easier if I got my things and examined Abigail in the car?' I asked. 'I know it isn't as private as a consulting room but it might be easier for her?'

Sarah looked relieved. 'That would be so helpful, wouldn't it, Abigail?' Abigail continued to scream and kick at her father.

I got my things and returned to the car. It turned out Abigail did have a chest infection and needed antibiotics which I prescribed for her.

Sadly, over the week her condition worsened despite the medication, and she ended up in hospital with a serious pneumonia. This had triggered off her epileptic seizures and she had to be sedated and put in the children's intensive care unit for a while to stop her from fitting. She spent two weeks in hospital before coming home.

I thought about this for a good while afterwards. It is always difficult as a doctor to be the last person to see a patient, offer them treatment, and for them to get worse and not better. It is especially difficult when the patient is a vulnerable child. I didn't sleep very well during the time Abigail was in hospital; I came into work and the first thing I would do each morning was check to see if her records indicated she had come home. When she finally did come home, I decided to call the parents to see how they were. Secretly, I was also calling in an attempt to vindicate myself. Although I had been over and over my examination findings and recognised there were no signs of pneumonia at the time, I still felt guilty. After all, this case was very similar to that of my friend Daniel's, where the child had died and he had been faced with an official complaint.

'Hi, it's Dr Khan,' I said when Sarah answered the phone. 'I was just ringing to see how Abigail was doing after her stay in hospital.'

'It was difficult, Dr Khan. One of us had to stay with her all the time, but she is home now and that's the important thing.'

Unless you have had a child in hospital, it is difficult to understand the impact it has on a parent's life. Unlike in times gone by, parents are now actively encouraged to stay with their children when in hospital. This eases anxiety for both the child and the parent. Sarah had done most of the hospital stays, but it had meant Michael had had to take time off work to look after their other daughter, Emily. Sarah told me that Michael was a self-employed electrician, so taking the last two weeks off work meant the family had had no income during that period, aside from the carer's allowance they were getting for Abigail. It had put a considerable financial pressure on the family.

'Of course, Abigail's health is our priority, but I won't pretend it wasn't difficult, Dr Khan,' Sarah had said.

'I hope you don't mind me asking, Mrs Lewis, but when you came to the surgery with Abigail, you looked like you had been crying. Was everything okay?' This had been playing on my mind ever since that day.

There was a pause on the other end.

'It had been a difficult morning,' Sarah said quietly.

'Oh I'm sorry, is it something I can help with?'

'We were tired, that's all. We had been awake with Abigail for most of the night, and were hoping we could get her seen early. When we brought Abigail into the waiting room it was so crowded she got very stressed and started screaming. Everybody was looking at us, so we thought it would be better if we waited in the car.' Sarah sounded like she was on the verge of tears again. 'People don't understand how hard it can be with Abigail. She is such a lovely child, but it can be hard.'

Chapter 12

I thought about what Sarah had just said. It made sense. Although we say we accommodate our vulnerable patients, were we actually doing this? What adjustments had the practice made in order to help Abigail and her family navigate our systems in a way that made their lives easier? The honest answer was none.

'She is getting bigger now,' Sarah continued. 'When she was younger we could just carry her around like any other child. It was easier, nobody would know she wasn't like all the other babies. Now she is older it is harder to get her to do the things she doesn't want to do. People still stare at us when we are out, Dr Khan. Especially if she is crying or shouting. I know it's not their fault, but they wouldn't do that if it was a baby who was crying.' Sarah was crying herself now. 'It has been a difficult few days, I'm sorry.'

'Don't be sorry,' I said. 'I just wish we could have made it easier for you when you visited that day.'

'We couldn't have waited three hours there, it just wouldn't have worked,' she replied.

'Mrs Lewis, would you mind telling me what *would* have made it easier to visit us?'

That question had led to where I was today, waiting for my next photoshoot despite the dark circles under my eyes. Sarah Lewis had helped us design a new system to help those with learning disabilities. We were going to have a set of stock photos for them to keep on their phones or tablets so they could familiarise themselves with our faces. This way we wouldn't be complete strangers when they came in. We also had a designated 'quiet' area of our waiting room as well as reminders put on these patients' notes to prioritise them when they needed appointments at certain times.

It had helped with Abigail's subsequent visits and was now being rolled out to all children and adults who would benefit from it.

These kinds of things are referred to as 'reasonable adjustments' in the NHS. They ensure that all patients have an equal access to healthcare no matter what their background and ensure those who are vulnerable are flagged up.

That night I made a reasonable adjustment to my social calendar, and cooked dinner for Robert when I got home. He told me Catherine had had a heart attack and would be staying in hospital for at least a week. He also told me they had moved into their current home over forty years ago and this was the first time he had spent a night away from her. I promised I would check on him regularly during the week and he promised to keep me updated on Catherine's condition.

Now it was 23 December and the festive season was fast approaching. As I logged into my computer that morning, I received a message from one of our health visitors. She had been to visit a single mum with four young children and had disclosed that the children would not be receiving any Christmas presents this year as there simply wasn't enough money in the household. It wasn't a medical problem of any sort, but the health visitor was signing off for the Christmas period and didn't want to take that particular bit of information with her. So here it was, in my inbox.

A lot of the staff were off for Christmas, and it only those of us who don't have children, those whose children were now adults or those who didn't get their holiday requests in on time holding the fort. I sit very firmly in that last category. I never understood people who can put in a whole year's holiday at the start of January. To be honest, I was a bit envious of them.

Chapter 12

It wasn't so bad working Christmas week. There was a festive buzz in the air, we could wear our silly Christmas jumpers (something I stopped doing a long time ago, when I realised wearing a hideous jumper where Rudolph's nose is a huge red pompom is totally inappropriate when you're telling someone about their cancer diagnosis), and for some reason it was the only week over the winter period when patients' demands for appointments were low. All my organised colleagues wouldn't be so smug when they came back to work at the start of January and there was a surge in people wanting appointments, I told myself; I would be sunning myself in Tenerife at that point.

I printed off the email and took it to see Nicola, one of our receptionists. We both deliberated over what we should do. We thought about ringing social services to see if they could help, but we knew this would be futile. They would be inundated with requests for getting people into care over the Christmas period and this would feature very low on their priority list. The fact that these children had a roof over their heads was enough for now as far as social services were concerned. Nicola suggested contacting a children's charity but couldn't get an answer from the local one we tried. In the end, we decided to send an email to all our staff asking if anyone would want to donate some money towards buying the two boys some Christmas presents. Nicola and I planned to nip out to the local supermarket at lunchtime, buy some gifts and hand-deliver them to their home.

By this time I was a partner at our practice. This means that as well as being a GP there, I own part of the business and the contract we have with the NHS. Generally, in the UK, GP practices are small organisations owned by a group of GPs, managers and other healthcare professionals. They hold a contract with the government and the NHS to provide primary care services to their patients. Although we work for and with the NHS, as a GP partner I am an independent worker and employer. As part of our contract we employ our staff ourselves. With this in mind, I knew that, financially, Christmas would be a tight time of year for a lot of our non-clinical staff. They don't get paid huge amounts and taking into account the pressure Christmas already puts on families, I wasn't expecting them to be able to contribute much to these children.

I was wrong. Within two hours all the staff, both clinical and non-clinical, had donated over two hundred pounds. Nicola and I were overwhelmed.

After morning surgery, we sent a 'thank you' email to everyone and made our way to the supermarket to buy gifts. We decided to get a mix of toys and clothes for them.

'If they don't have enough money for presents, they won't have enough money for decent clothes either,' Nicola said. I agreed.

We had taken the address of the family with us and planned to drop the presents off on our way back to the surgery. I put the details into the satnav and we were on our way. It was close to the surgery so hopefully we wouldn't be too late getting back.

When you work in inner cities, you think you would get used to seeing the kind of poverty people can still live in. You don't get used to it at all; your heart still breaks with every encounter. When I try to describe this to some of my friends who work in larger, more affluent cities or in the country they find it hard to believe.

The street was on a slope, and there were terraced houses on either side. The family lived in one of the centre houses. The upstairs window was broken and a black bin liner had been taped over the top of it. The front door was made of plastic that was made to look like wood, the letterbox had been taped shut and there was a sign above it saying *'Beware of the Dog'*. The downstairs window had no curtains, allowing us to see all the way inside. The number of the house had been spray-painted in black on the wall.

I knocked on the door. No answer. I tried again. Still nothing.

Nicola cupped her hands against the downstairs window and pressed her face against it, checking to see if there was anyone inside.

'Nobody there,' she said. 'JODIE!' She shouted looking up at the bedroom window. 'We're from the doctors' surgery, it's Dr Khan and Nicola.'

I noticed a quick movement upstairs in the window. I knocked hard again on the front door. 'Jodie, it's Dr Khan. Can you please open the door?' I said loudly.

We waited a few more minutes. A young lady appeared from the house next door, wearing her dressing gown despite it being well after lunchtime. She was smoking a cigarette. I recognised her: Shelley Eastwood, one of our patients.

'All right, Dr Khan?' she said, cigarette still in mouth. 'After Jodie, are you?' She took a drag from her cigarette and exhaled a thick puff of smoke.

'Hi, Ms Eastwood, yes I am. Is she in?' I asked.

'She's in,' she drawled. 'Probably thinks you're with the social, so won't open the door.'

'Well we're actually here to drop off some Christmas presents for the children,' I said. 'Do you know how I can get that message to her?'

Shelley looked at me suspiciously before nodding and disappearing back inside, presumably to phone her neighbour.

Nicola and I waited outside. It was getting chilly. I hadn't planned on standing outside for this long, and the good vibes we had had about playing Santa and delivering gifts were beginning to dissipate.

'She's coming,' Shelley said, returning to her front step to finish her cigarette.

The sound of a key turning in a lock came from behind Jodie's front door. The door opened a fraction and Jodie peered through.

'Yeah?' she said.

'Jodie, it's Dr Khan from the surgery. This is Nicola. We heard your boys didn't have anything for Christmas, so we have come to drop something off for them,' I said gently. She looked like a timid mouse from behind the door.

Jodie opened the door. 'Come in.'

We went inside. The door opened straight into the living room. It had a sofa and a small white plastic table and chairs that looked like they were designed to be garden furniture. The carpet looked like it was once cream-coloured but now was a dull shade of brown. A dog lay asleep on the floor, he opened one eye to look at us, then rolled over and went back to sleep. He didn't quite match up to the *'Beware of the Dog'* sign outside.

'We had a message from the health visitor, Suzie, this morning,' I said to Jodie, who looked terrified. 'She said the boys wouldn't have any Christmas presents this year, so we did a little whip-round at the practice and bought them some nice things.'

I don't know what I was expecting, probably for Jodie to burst into tears or at least show some kind of emotion. But I expect people showing her kindness may have been unknown territory to her, and she simply continued to look stunned.

Chapter 12

'Are the boys at school, Jodie?' Nicola asked. She nodded. 'Well, that's good, you can hide the presents and give them to them on Christmas morning.' She handed Jodie the two full carrier bags.

Jodie took them cautiously, as if they might explode. 'Thank you,' she said, still unsure.

'Well, we'd better get back to the surgery. Merry Christmas, Jodie. I hope the boys like the gifts.'

Nicola and I drove back to work. Despite Jodie's less-than-enthusiastic response, we were still feeling positive for having delivered the presents. We returned to the surgery with a bit of a spring in our step and fed the news back to our staff.

I imagined Jodie's four boys opening their Christmas presents on Christmas Day and was filled with a warm glow. I was also really proud of our practice for coming together like we had done.

Two weeks later, I returned from Tenerife and back to work. I paraded my new tan around the building, paying particular attention to those who had taken Christmas and New Year off. As with any job, the minute you get back to work and log on it feels like you have never been away. I prepared an especially large cup of coffee before I decided to tackle my emails. Among them was one from Suzie, the health visitor. Jodie's boys had been taken into care. Her previous partner was a convicted sex offender and was not supposed to come near the children. Unfortunately, she had succumbed to his charms over the holidays and had let him stay in the house. Social services had got wind of it via Shelley, their neighbour. The children were now staying with a foster family.

My heart sank as I read the email. It was easy to be angry at Jodie, but I knew things were never as straightforward as they seemed on the surface for these families. Their lives can be quite chaotic and what would seem like an easy choice for some is not quite so easy for others. Suzie's email said the boys had been taken away just after New Year. I just hoped that they had managed to have a few moments of cheer on Christmas morning, playing with the toys we had bought for them.

It was hard not to compare Jodie's parenting style to that of Sarah and Michael Lewis, who were selflessly sacrificing everything to do what was best for their daughter, despite all her special needs and challenges. But I realised it was unhelpful to compare the two families. Who knew what Jodie had been through herself to lead her to letting that ex back into her life? Everyone was just doing the best they could.

I debated whether or not to tell the rest of the team about what had happened. They had all been so generous in their contributions and there was a real sense of pride about what we had done in a short space of time. I decided I had to tell them; it wasn't my information to keep back. I sent an email. Everybody was sad about it, but what was sadder was that very few people were surprised.

Chapter Thirteen

It's part of a GP's job to have difficult conversations. Rarely a day goes by that I don't have to break some bad news, or try to persuade someone into healthier lifestyle choices (often to great resistance), or pacify an angry patient who has become infuriated with the waiting time for a referral. When we train to be GPs, we spend years learning our way around the mysteries of the human body, but once we are practising, our skill with words is almost as important as our skill with a stethoscope. This is never more the case then when dealing with someone in chronic pain, which can bring with it a whole host of other problems such as depression and painkiller addiction. As such it needs to be handled with extreme sensitivity.

One such sufferer was a 38-year-old lady called Ellie Whelon, whose name came up on my list early one morning. I called her in, the inevitable 'door knock' came and I shouted, 'Come in.' The handle moved and the door opened ajar and then closed again. I looked up, and the same thing happened again. I got up and went to open the door.

'Thank you,' Ellie said as I ushered her in. 'These doors are heavy and I struggle to balance on my crutches and push it open.' It was true – they were weighted fire safety doors. Ellie hobbled in and took a seat.

'Hi, Ms Whelon, I'm Dr Khan. How can I help?' I hadn't met Ellie before. According to her notes she saw one of the other GPs at the practice regularly but she was currently on holiday so today Ellie had been booked in with me.

'I don't suppose you've read my notes?' Ellie said, gesturing to the computer. I had read some of them. She suffered from longstanding back pain, which had started six years ago after a fall down some stairs. She had been taken to hospital at the time with a suspected fractured vertebra. The CT scans cleared her of this, but did pick up some small disc bulges in her spine. The problem with disc bulges is that a lot of people have them and sometimes they cause symptoms and sometimes they don't. Ellie's pain had not subsided with time as we had expected; in fact, it had got worse, though the exact nature of it was unclear.

'I had a look through them, yes. Tell me how you are today.' As I hadn't met Ellie before, I wanted to hear it from her rather than read it in the notes. Ellie was trying to hook her crutches onto the corner of the table to stop them from ending up on the floor. Each time she did, they would slide along the table edge before she caught them and tried again. 'Here, let me,' I said, taking the crutches and hooking them to the back of an empty chair. 'There, they shouldn't go anywhere now.'

'I've come about my back. It's no better with the new tablets I was given last time. I just don't know what to do about it,' Ellie said.

'Okay, tell me about how your back feels,' I said gently.

'It's constantly painful. It doesn't matter if I sit still or move around, it is always there. If I put too much pressure on my legs just walking, the pain is excruciating, that's why I've got them,' Ellie said, pointing at the crutches. 'I am not sleeping. I can't even sit on the sofa for too long but then getting up hurts too.' Ellie was on the verge of tears now. Every GP keeps a box of tissues handy, so I took one and passed it to her. 'Thank you,' she said, wiping the tears away before they spilled out onto her cheeks.

Ellie's notes told me she had been referred to several specialists about her back over the last few years. She had initially seen a spinal consultant who felt physiotherapy to strengthen the muscles in her lower back was the best approach, in the hope they would absorb a lot of the pressure being put on her spine. This had had little effect, and she had subsequently been referred to see an anaesthetist who ran a specialised pain clinic. They had tried spinal injections, which had brought temporary relief but not for long enough to repeat the injections. To Ellie's distress, the anaesthetist had discharged her on the grounds that they were not making any improvements. She had then been seen by a rheumatologist in case there was a condition we were not thinking of that would account for her pain, but this had not been fruitful. All the tests and investigations had not unearthed a diagnosis and Ellie was left in the unenviable position of having 'medically unexplained symptoms'.

I chose my next words carefully.

'Ellie, I know you have been seen by a number of people who have helped us rule out some diagnoses and this may seem like a strange question, but tell me what worries you most about your pain.'

Ellie paused for thought. 'I am only thirty-eight years old. My daughter is nine and my son eleven. I can't play with them. I can't walk them to school any more. I don't want the rest of my life to be like this.'

It was a valid concern. I handed Ellie another tissue.

'What do you say to all the tests you have had so far? Are you worried that we have missed a diagnosis?' It was important for me to understand where Ellie was up to in her thought process.

'No, I know they don't show anything serious. To be honest, I have given up on finding the cause. I just want to be out of pain and to live a normal life again.' Ellie had stopped crying now. She was focused.

'Does the pain ever affect your mood?' I asked. Ellie nodded. 'How low can it make you feel?' Ellie didn't say anything. I tried a different approach. 'Sometimes, Ellie, patients with longstanding pain can feel very low to a point where they wish they were not here anymore. Have you ever had any thoughts like this?' I maintained my eye contact with her. She nodded.

As clinicians, we understand that any chronic illness that affects a patient's quality of life will have a detrimental effect on their mood. We have to ask the question about deliberate self-harm as that qualifies as a medical emergency and needs prompt treatment. It is now an old-fashioned idea to think that asking about thoughts of self-harm may trigger someone to hurt themselves.

'Ellie, have you had any thoughts or made any plans about hurting yourself?'

Ellie shook her head vigorously. 'I would never do that to my kids. I want to get better for them, not make it worse.' She sounded resolute.

'Have you ever taken anything that has helped with your pain?' I asked, satisfied with her previous answer.

'Just the injections, but they only lasted two weeks and then the pain came back.'

'I am glad you have come to see me today, Ellie, and I will do my best to help you. But before I do, was there anything you were hoping I would do?'

Chapter 13

'I don't know if there is any other medication you can give me to help with the pain because the tablets I am on now don't seem to touch it,' Ellie said. 'You know, Dr Khan, I used to run, like really run. I ran for my school and then for the county. After having the kids, I didn't have time for all of that, but I still ran for my running club and I would compete in races with them. I haven't run in six years.' Ellie was no longer emotional; she was just making me understand how much the pain had changed her life.

'I am a runner too,' I said. 'I think I would struggle if I couldn't run on a regular basis.'

'There must be something I can take for the pain, something I haven't tried before.'

Ellie was already on three different painkillers. Her notes showed she had tried others before and they had been ineffective.

For doctors the art of pain relief is like a game where it feels as if the goal posts are always shifting. Getting it right involves having frank and difficult conversations with our patients. When I qualified as a GP, there were a number of painkilling medications to choose from, but over time we have gained a better understanding of the pitfalls of our 'go to' medication and the advice has changed. The main group of drugs in this discussion is the opioids. This includes medication such as codeine, tramadol and morphine. We know this group of medication has a beneficial effect in short-term pain relief but in the long term patients can build up a tolerance, requiring higher doses to achieve the same effect. They can also be highly addictive. Alarming statistics from the US and the UK show huge numbers of people taking these medications long term, on prescription from their doctors. Clinicians now avoid prescribing these medications in the long term and to try to wean those who are on them on to smaller doses.

But where does that leave the patient? Most people who are taking these medications are doing so on the advice of their doctor and have been getting regular prescriptions for them. They have trusted their doctor and now the rug is being pulled out from under their feet. They are getting phone calls saying they must reduce the number of these tablets they take every day and that we aim to stop them eventually. Any perceived problems during this weaning-off process are put down to 'withdrawal' symptoms and they are told to grit their teeth and get through it until they wear off. There are also very few safe alternatives. Most of the newer medication used to treat pain can also be addictive or have side effects that are unacceptable to patients.

It is difficult for both sides.

I have long found dealing with chronic pain a hugely challenging issue so I attended a talk on it one night held by a GP who had a special interest in managing such cases.

'Think of pain like a pillow you are carrying around,' she had said. 'Carrying around the weight of the pillow is manageable. But when the pain causes depression it is like adding a heavy book onto that pillow. Then the sleepless nights are another heavy book on top of that. Losing contact with friends as a result of the pain is another book. Then with all these books as well as the pillow, the pain becomes unmanageable. We have to make our patients get back to just the pillow again.'

I'm not particularly philosophical, but I saw the point she was trying to make. However, I imagined that if I likened Ellie's pain to a pillow and a series of books, I might get smacked in the face.

Chapter 13

'Ellie, you mentioned the pain keeping you up at night. Do you worry about not being able to sleep?'

'Yes. I guess the pain feels worse at night or at least I feel more alone with the pain at night. My husband is asleep and I don't want to wake him so I have to lie very still. When I turn to try to get more comfortable it is like an electric shock in my spine and it is all I can do to stop crying out. The nights feel long.'

I listened sympathetically but it was time for me to talk frankly. 'Sometimes, Ellie, it gets to a point where giving you stronger and stronger pain relief is not the right approach. I very much believe your pain is bad and is having detrimental consequences on your life,' I said. I was being very direct with Ellie now; for this approach to work I needed her to come with me. 'The effect on your mood, your sleep and your family can make the pain feel so much worse, and in a way we have to get you to learn how to manage the pain without it affecting these other things.'

Ellie paused. 'How can we do that without taking the pain away?' she asked.

'We have to get you to think about the pain differently. It is there and we know it is there, and we also know there is no sinister cause for it. Somehow we have to make it so it is no longer the most important thing in your life,' I said, trying to read Ellie's reaction.

'Are you saying all this pain is in my head, Dr Khan?' Ellie said slowly.

'No, not at all. It is very real pain, but managing it might involve trying to tackle the psychological effects of the pain rather than the pain itself.'

'How can we do that?' Ellie asked. She seemed relieved that I believed her when she said the pain was real.

'Rather than throw more medication at you I would like to refer you to the Living with Pain team. They see patients who have chronic pain and help them manage it without the need for medication,' I said.

'And they won't think it's all in my head?' Ellie asked.

'Absolutely not. They see patients with long-term pain all the time and use cognitive behavioural therapy to help them manage it and live their lives at the same time. They will help you get back to the things you enjoy doing. Would you like me to refer you to them?'

'How long would I be waiting to be seen?' she asked. That was the million-dollar question. The NHS was overwhelmed with referrals in all its departments, but with our shift away from prescribing painkilling tablets, the Living with Pain team had particularly long waiting lists.

'Hopefully not too long,' I said vaguely. It was the best I could do; we could debate the shortfalls of our wonderful NHS services until the cows came home but it wouldn't make any difference. Every referral had an unpleasant wait time attached to it.

'And what do I do in the meantime?' Ellie asked. Another difficult question.

'Some of the things you have told me today suggest you may be suffering from depression because of your pain. Is that something you've thought about?'

Ellie nodded. 'Yes, I guess I think about it a lot, though I have never said it out loud before.'

'Would you want to try an antidepressant or talking therapy, perhaps?' I asked. 'Just to lift your mood?' To be perfectly honest, the wait time for counselling – now called talking therapy – was also pretty lengthy, so either way poor Ellie had a long wait ahead of her.

Chapter 13

'Are antidepressants not addictive like the painkillers?'

I shook my head. 'Some of the older ones were, but the newer ones have fewer side effects and patients can come off them much more easily.' Ellie didn't say anything. 'Why don't I give you some information about them and you can come back to see me after you have given it some thought?'

'Okay, that's if I can get an appointment.' Another comment I didn't have a solution for.

I gave Ellie the information sheet about antidepressants and helped her with her crutches. She thanked me as she left, but I wasn't sure I had got her completely on side with the Living with Pain team.

I felt sorry for Ellie; like all my chronic pain patients she was stuck between the problems of the medication and the pain itself. I understood why patients felt the risks of addiction and tolerance were worth some respite from the pain, but the truth was the tablets would only have limited benefit and we would either need to have the same conversation again in the future or increase the doses to dangerous levels to achieve the same effect. It was a problem that doctors themselves had created and that patients were now paying the price for.

Difficult conversations are hard enough with any patient, but of course they are harder still when they are with a child.

One of the receptionists came to see me early the next morning. Wendy and Emily had been in wanting to see me but I was already fully booked. They were asking if they could be seen as an urgent extra on the end of my clinic. I said yes.

'I think she had a panic attack,' Wendy said about Emily when they came in. 'She just said she wanted to go home and started crying. Then she said her chest hurt.'

Wendy and Emily had been at funeral earlier that day. It was for one of Emily's friends at the hospice, a seven-year-old boy called Malik who had been diagnosed with lymphoma last year. I didn't know him, but Emily had talked about him before. Because they were the same age, they had done everything together at the hospice. Unfortunately, he had become very sick with an infection and, because his immune system was so weak, it had overwhelmed him and he had died three days later.

They had been at Malik's funeral when Emily had had her panic attack. I checked her heart and lungs; they all seemed fine.

'Emily, do you want to talk about it?' I said to her. Emily was now seven years old and understood more about her heart condition.

She stayed silent.

'Emily, tell Dr Khan what you told me,' Wendy said to her. Still nothing.

'You know, Emily, it's okay to ask questions. Especially on days like today. I imagine you have a lot of questions,' I said.

She still didn't say anything.

'Do you miss Malik?' I asked. She nodded her head. 'It's not fair, is it?' She shook her head and whispered something, but I didn't quite catch it. 'I'm sorry, Emily, I didn't hear that.'

'Am I going to die?' she said a little louder.

I looked at Wendy who nodded at me. It was a question I was used to being asked by my adult patients who had new cancer diagnoses, but never by a child. It broke my heart. It would be a difficult question for any doctor to answer.

'Nobody knows when any of us are going to die,' I started slowly. 'But I can promise you this, I will always do my very best to look after you and make you better. And you have all those doctors at the hospital looking after you too.'

Chapter 13

'The doctors and nurses at the hospital are very nice to you, aren't they, Emily?' Wendy said. Emily nodded.

'And you have your mum; she loves you so much and will never leave your side,' I said. Emily smiled.

'Will you look after my mum if I die?' Emily asked, louder this time. Wendy stopped and looked at her. I don't think Emily had said this out loud to her before. She bit down on her lip to try to stop herself from crying.

'Of course I will, and your sisters,' I said.

We talked a little while longer before they left. I took a pause before calling in my next patient. I just needed a minute.

Chapter Fourteen

I had woken up to a text from Alison Daniels. She had lost her car keys and needed me to pick her up on the way to work. I texted her back saying I was happy to, but it would be an early pick-up as I had planned to get in first thing and clear some paperwork.

Now I was watching Alison blow-dry and straighten her hair in my clinic room.

'The lighting is better in this room than in mine,' she said as she pulled at her hair with the straightening irons. 'I'm trying to grow my hair so I can put it into a ponytail.'

Alison had been trying to grow her hair for as long as I could remember. She usually got it to her jawline before she gave up and got it all cut off. It was cycle that repeated itself every six months.

'I used to have long hair when I was a health visitor,' she said, looking in the mirror.

Alison, now an advanced nurse practitioner, had a background in health visiting and paediatric nursing. One of my favourite stories she told me was when she used to visit her South Asian patients. She said she would visit these families with young children at home and she could hear the kids shout upstairs to their mums: 'Mum, the Gauri is here!' Alison always laughed at this point. Gauri was Punjabi for 'white lady'. The mums would then open the door and greet her like family.

'Hi Alison, lovely to see you.'

'Don't "hi Alison" me,' she would say. 'I heard you calling me the Gauri through the door!'

'Oh no, Alison, we don't mean you when we say that. You're all right, it's the other Gauris we're talking about.'

'Come on, let's have a look at this gorgeous baby,' Alison would say, brushing the casual racism under the carpet.

'You know, Amir, if I ever write a book I will call it *The Gauri is Coming*,' she had laughed.

Now, satisfied with her hair, she stood in front of the mirror applying eyeliner while I went through the 'task list'.

Tasks are messages sent by other people through the computer system asking you to act on something. Usually it's asking for a prescription or an opinion on a clinical case, other times it comes from people outside the practice, like district nurses or health visitors, asking us to review a patient.

I had a task from the palliative care team about a patient I knew called Rosie Price.

Rosie Price was a very sad case. She was a 27-year-old woman who had been diagnosed with cervical cancer two years ago. We thought we had caught it in time and referred her to see the gynae-oncologists at the hospital. After having extensive surgery, she had several rounds of chemotherapy, which left her immune system in tatters. She had had to be admitted to hospital as an emergency on two occasions with a condition known as neutro-penic sepsis, which meant the white cells in her body that form part of her natural immune response were so depleted she had no defence against the infection that was now trying to overwhelm her body. The chemotherapy had also left her on a whole host of heart medication.

Despite all of this, around twelve months ago it felt like we were winning. The specialists at the hospital felt they had turned a corner with her and she was showing signs of being cancer-free. But the relief was short-lived: a follow-up scan showed traces of the cancer had spread through her lymph nodes to her bladder, liver and lungs. She was offered further chemotherapy, but it was in an effort to prolong her life rather than cure the cancer, so she had opted not to go through it again and was now being kept comfortable at home.

I was nominated as Rosie's lead GP. All our patients with serious palliative diagnoses have a 'lead GP' assigned to them so they get continued care from a clinician who knows them.

I visited Rosie at least once every two weeks. For a clinician to be able to fill out a death certificate for a patient they need to have seen them within two weeks of their death. If this has not been the case it can get very messy, involving the coroner and trying to explain why a patient does not need a post-mortem.

Rosie had lived with her boyfriend prior to the diagnosis, but as things got worse she moved in with her mum and cousin. She had split up with her boyfriend a few weeks before the move, supposedly by mutual arrangement, but I suspect she knew how serious her prognosis was and felt she needed to let him go.

The task stated that the palliative care nurses wanted me to call them that morning. It was too early to call yet, as the day-time staff wouldn't have arrived. I would call them later.

Alison had finished getting ready and was packing away her hair dryer and make-up.

'You okay to give me a lift back this evening, Amir?' she said, taking one last look in the mirror.

'Of course,' I replied as she left.

It was now 8 a.m. and patients were beginning to get booked into my clinic. Some of the names I recognised and others were new to me.

Chapter 14

There was a knock on the door from Nicola, our reception manager.

'Hi, Nicola, is everything okay?' I asked. At this time in the morning it was very unusual to get a visit from one of our reception team; it was usually 'all hands on deck' as the phone calls to book appointments came in thick and fast.

'There may be a slight issue, and I am not quite sure what to do,' Nicola said, sitting down. 'Have you been spraying perfume in here?' she added, sniffing the air.

'Alison. She got ready in here, something to do with the light apparently,' I replied. 'What's up?'

'I don't want to alarm you, but take a look at your first patient,' Nicola said slowly.

I looked at my screen. My first patient was a man named William Butler. I didn't recognise the name, so I put a quick search for my name in his records which confirmed I had never consulted with him before.

'He is a relatively new patient,' Nicola said. 'He was waiting in the queue this morning along with some other people. The thing is, one of the other patients disclosed to the receptionists at the front desk that they saw him hide a hammer up his sleeve.'

'A hammer?' I said, taken aback.

'That's what they said. We don't know if it's true but we weren't sure what to do.'

'Let me just have a quick look through his notes.' I scanned through his previous consultations at his last surgery and his hospital letters, but there was nothing in there that would suggest he had any kind of psychiatric past or previous history of violence. 'It's all pretty straightforward stuff,' I said to Nicola.

'Yeah, I had a look through his notes too,' she said, sitting back in the chair. 'Shall we call the police?'

I thought about it – there was definitely a risk associated with consulting a patient with a concealed weapon. But we didn't know what Mr Butler's intentions were and we only had another patient's word for it, so calling the police felt a bit like overkill.

'Probably not yet,' I said.

'Do you want me to stay in the room with you while you see him?' Nicola said.

I thought about it. It was very nice of Nicola to offer to stay but it didn't sit well with me. I knew how busy reception was first thing in the morning, plus there was the male chauvinistic part of me who felt I shouldn't need a woman to protect me should I get attacked by a man with a hammer.

'Why don't I see him and ask him directly about the hammer? I'll keep one hand on the panic button,' I said.

'Are you sure? We could get Gerard in, if you prefer.' Nicola must have read my mind.

'No, I'm sure it'll be fine,' I said, not sure at all.

'Okay, well I might wait outside your room just in case,' Nicola said as she left. I was secretly grateful.

William Butler had told the reception staff he wanted to see the GP because of a headache. They had written this down in his notes. I buzzed for him to come in. He was thirty-two years old but looked older. His hair was a dirty shade of blond and needed a wash, and he wore a thick green jacket which made it impossible to tell if there was anything hidden up his sleeve. His hands looked dirty from soil, like he had just come in from doing some gardening. The strangest part was that he was wearing an eye patch, like a pirate. Trying to read his intentions by looking at just one of his eyes made it all the more difficult. He sat in the chair opposite me.

Chapter 14

I didn't know whether I should ask him about the hammer outright or perhaps get to know him first, gain his trust and then ask him. If I asked him outright and he turned out to be a dangerous man, I might risk angering him and provoking an attack. I decided to wait.

'Hi, Mr Butler, my name is Dr Khan. How can I help?' I said, trying to sound as friendly as possible. Nobody could wallop someone who sounded so cheerful over the head with a hammer.

'I've come about my headaches,' William said. 'I was on some medication for them in my last surgery and I needed a repeat prescription.' William Butler sounded perfectly normal.

'Sure, tell me about your headaches,' I said.

'I've had them for years. The last doctor told me they were migraines, and gave me some tablets to take daily to prevent them.' Again, William sounded like a perfectly sane person. His story married up with what was written in his notes.

'Do the tablets help when you take them?'

'Yes, provided I don't have a break from them, they work. If I stop taking them, the headaches come back,' William said.

'Do you suffer from any mood problems because of your headaches?' I asked cautiously. Perhaps William was suffering from a sudden psychosis that had not previously manifested.

'No, not really,' he said.

'Do you ever hear voices in your head telling you to do things?' I asked carefully. He looked confused. 'Just routine questions we ask everyone,' I said (everyone with a hammer tucked up their sleeve).

'No, of course not,' he said, frowning.

'Do the headaches get so bad you think about harming your-self, or other people?' I continued.

'Dr Khan, I don't mean to be rude but these are not the same questions the last doctor asked me when I told him about my headaches,' William said, looking slightly agitated.

The last thing I wanted to do was upset a man with a con-cealed weapon. I decided to change tack.

'Sorry, Mr Butler, it's just that you are new here. I can see from your records you were prescribed propranolol for your headaches. I am happy to re-prescribe it but I just need to check your blood pressure first.' I had him now; he would have to take off his jacket in order for me to check his blood pressure. 'I just need to get to the top of your arm.' I made a show of unfolding the blood pressure cuff and putting my stethoscope round my neck.

William Butler nodded, unbuttoned his jacket and placed it on the back of his chair. He wore a waffled grey jumper under-neath and there was definitely something strange about the way he was holding his left arm. I looked closer – yes, there seemed to be something hidden underneath the sleeve of his jumper.

He used his left arm awkwardly to hold his jumper in place while he pulled his right arm out.

'It'll be easier if we use the left arm; the cuff doesn't stretch all the way to your right one,' I said. This was true. The blood pressure machine was fixed to the wall and Mr Butler's left arm was closest to it.

He glanced at the blood pressure machine and nodded.

He then used his right arm to pull out a large hammer from under his left sleeve, which he placed carefully on the desk. I looked at the hammer and then at Mr Butler who was waiting expectantly to have his blood pressure taken.

Chapter 14

'Mr Butler, that is a hammer,' I said slowly.

'Yes it is.'

'You cannot bring that into the surgery. It is classed as a weapon.' I had one hand hovering over my panic button.

'A weapon? It's a hammer not a weapon,' he said, sounding incredulous. 'Are you going to take my blood pressure or not? This is the strangest doctor's appointment I have ever had.'

Before I could answer there was a knock on the door and Nicola came in with Gerard, our caretaker, behind her.

'Heard a commotion, just checking everything is all right,' Nicola said, giving me a knowing look.

'Commotion? There wasn't a commotion!' Mr Butler said.

To be fair to Mr Butler, there hadn't been anything like a commotion.

'Thanks, Nicola, Mr Butler was just about to tell me why he thought it appropriate to bring a hammer into a doctor's office,' I said, sitting back in my chair and folding my arms. I was feeling more confident now that reinforcements had arrived.

'It's for my horse!' Mr Butler said, clearly confused about why there were three people in with him.

'Your horse?' Now it was my turn to be confused.

'Yes, my horse. It's what I've come in on today,' William said. 'He's in the park at the back of the surgery.'

'Why do you need a hammer to come in on a horse?' Nicola asked.

'I have to hammer in a post to the ground to tie him to.' We all must have looked at him blankly. 'To stop him running away.' William sounded exasperated.

'Right then, that explains things,' I said after a brief pause. 'Thank you, Nicola, thank you, Gerard. I think I can take it from here.' Nicola looked embarrassed as she left, Gerard still looked baffled. 'Well, there seems to have been some confusion, Mr Butler. Another patient reported you had a hammer hidden up your sleeve and we weren't sure of your intentions.'

'That explains some of those questions you were asking earlier,' he said.

'Yes, it's not often we have patients arrive on horseback,' I said.

'He's attached to a cart. I sit in the cart not on his back,' William said.

'Yes, well that is also a first for us. I am sorry for the confusion. Shall we get back to checking your blood pressure?' I said, desperate to change the subject.

William took the misunderstanding well and left with his prescription for propranolol.

My next patient was more familiar, Wendy Ashworth. The appointment note stated she wanted to talk to me about Emily.

Emily was ten years old now. Things were not going well. She had outgrown the shunt that had been placed in her heart when she was five. Emily's heart had to work harder than a normal person's to transport oxygenated blood around her body, and as a result of working so hard over the last ten years it was starting to weaken and become less effective. Her lungs were also working harder as a result and the blood pressure within her lungs was starting to get to worryingly high levels.

She was finding that fluid that should have been circulating around her body was starting to build in places it shouldn't. Her feet and ankles began to swell. Fluid built up on her lungs, making her even more short of breath. She had missed weeks of school and was lagging behind the other children in her year group. Wendy soldiered on, taking her to her hospital appointments, staying with her on the ward when she was too ill to be at home. It was beginning to take its toll on both of them.

'They've said she needs a heart transplant,' Wendy said. She had come alone. 'They've put her on the list, and it's now just a case of waiting for a heart to become available.'

We both knew what that meant. Emily would need a child's heart who was around the same age as her. A brave family somewhere in England would have to make one of the most difficult decisions in the world at the darkest time of their lives.

I had seen the organ donation team at the hospital. I couldn't imagine how difficult that job must be, talking to families in times of grief about organ donation. I understood how important it was, how there was a shortage of organs available for those who needed it, how children and adults were dying because they hadn't received the organ they so desperately needed. Those conversations that team were having were saving lives every single day.

'If she doesn't get a heart soon, we might lose her,' she said. She allowed herself a moment to cry, then wiped away the tears. 'I'm sorry.'

'I think if anyone is allowed to have a cry, it's you.' There wasn't much more I could say. We had come to a dead end with Emily's treatment options.

'She gets short of breath just moving from one room to another. We have to keep her moving or her ankles will swell further. It's just so hard to know what's the right thing to do,' Wendy continued. 'I think we are all just so tired.'

Emily was also waking up at night short of breath. She was on medication that helped shift some of the fluid and controlled the rate at which her heart beat, but they were still struggling.

Wendy had always resisted any offer of medication to help with her mood, but today she felt differently.

'I think I might be suffering from depression, Dr Khan,' she said flatly. 'I have done everything I could possibly do. I take her to every hospital appointment; we've been to Newcastle, Sheffield, London, Bristol, everywhere. I pray every night, I even started going to church again, but we still ended up here. I think we were always going to end up here.'

I didn't say anything.

'I feel hopeless.' She paused and looked up at me. 'I think she is going to die.'

'No, Wendy, we don't know that. That is what depression does to you, it makes you feel hopeless,' I said. 'Anyone would be suffering from mood problems if they had gone through everything you have been through.'

She looked at the floor, not saying anything.

'I know you have declined them in the past, but I really think you should consider taking some medication for your mood.'

She nodded. 'Yes, I think so too.'

Wendy promised to come and see me again in two weeks to see if the medication was helping. In turn, I asked her to let me know if they got that all-important phone call from the organ donation team, and she said she would.

As I was finishing typing up Wendy's notes, an instant message popped up on my screen telling me Philippa, the palliative care nurse, was on the phone for me. With everything that had gone on with Mr Butler, I had forgotten to ring her back.

We had a good working relationship with our palliative care nurses; to be honest they did most of the work when it came to looking after our palliative patients in the community. They would only ring us if they really had to, as they were more than capable of doing most things themselves.

'Hi Philippa, it's Amir. Sorry I haven't managed to ring you back, it's been one of those mornings,' I said, getting my apology in early.

'Don't worry, I'm used to chasing up GPs,' Phillipa said. 'I'm ringing regarding Rosie Price. The receptionist said you were her lead GP?'

'That's right.'

'There has been an issue with her medication, specifically her morphine,' Philippa continued. 'We are missing a box of it.'

'Missing? How do you mean?' I asked.

Sometimes, when we hand out prescriptions in general practice they would somehow get lost between the surgery and the pharmacy, or the patient would say they never received it. It was fairly easy to see if prescriptions had been dispensed by the pharmacists and issued to the patient, then we would have to have a conversation with the patient about what they had done with the medication. Moving to electronic prescribing and doing away with the green bits of paper had helped considerably as we could now track every prescription. Some medication, like those for blood pressure or asthma, we would replace quite easily, but there were others, specifically the addictive painkillers and sleeping tablets, which we would be reluctant to replace. I had lost count of the number of times a patient had said they had left their very addictive diazepam or gabapentin on the bus or that a 'friend' may have accidentally picked up their zopiclone and now they had none left. I had quickly become acquainted with the street value of all our addictive and highly sellable medication and took a very hard line with these stories.

'We had a box of ten vials delivered by the pharmacist two days ago,' Phillipa said. 'It was supposed to last a week. As always, we locked it in the controlled drugs safe in Rosie's home. When we were called in the night by her mum to administer her some because she was in pain, there was none there.' Philippa paused. 'It was just the morphine that was gone. Her cyclizine and halo-peridol were still there.'

Rosie's condition was now such that she was bedbound. Because she slipped in and out of consciousness, the way we assessed whether or not she was in pain was when the nurses changed her pad or dressings; at these moments they would check to see if she grimaced or made a sound suggesting we were not controlling her pain adequately.

The sad truth is cancer can cause terrible pain. As it spreads, it also grows, pressing on organs, nerves and pain receptors, inflicting pain that would be unimaginable to you and me. Rosie was getting the majority of her medication through a syringe driver, a device that continuously administered medication directly under her skin. This meant she always had a dose of pain relief, anti-sickness and relaxants to help her pain.

The vials Phillipa was referring to were the ones used to top up Rosie's medication in case she got breakthrough pain despite the medication in the syringe driver. Because of the nature of syringe driver medication, drugs like morphine had to be kept in a locked box, the keys to which only those who were administer-ing Rosie's medication had. This would normally be the palliative care nurses and the district nurses.

'You mean somebody removed them from the safe?' I said, unsure. 'How is that possible?'

'The lock was broken when we went in last night, and the morphine was gone,' Philippa said.

Chapter 14

'Broken? But there is only Rosie's mum and her cousin at home,' I said, still not quite there.

'Yes, that's right.'

I took a moment. I had to be sure I understood what was being said.

'Did anyone else visit the home in the last day or so? Friends? Family?' I asked.

'I've spoken with Mrs Price this morning, and she said Jack, Rosie's cousin, had his friend Mason round last night.' Phillipa stopped abruptly.

'Philippa?'

'Mrs Price and Jack are not registered at your practice, are they, Amir?'

'No, they're not,' I replied. 'Why?'

Technically, Rosie's mum's house was outside our practice boundary. When Rosie had lived with her boyfriend, their house had been within our boundary and so she was registered with us. When she had become too unwell to care for herself and moved in with her mum, we told her she could stay registered with us, which she had been happy about. Her mum and cousin were registered at a practice local to them.

'Mrs Price does the majority of Rosie's care,' Phillipa continued. 'She washes her, changes her pad, even some of the stuff we would normally do. She normally calls us early if she has any concerns about Rosie, but it's strange she didn't notice the lock to the safe had been broken. That is exactly the kind of thing she would notice.' It felt like Philippa was dropping a trail of breadcrumbs for me to follow, but I still wasn't getting it.

'Philippa, you don't think Mrs Price took the medication?' I said, shocked. I had met Mrs Price on several occasions, and never in a million years would I have thought she would steal controlled drugs.

'No, Amir, I don't. But we do have concerns about Jack. We know he smokes marijuana at the house, we can smell it when we go in and he has a history of drug use. It wouldn't be a giant leap to think he could have taken the morphine.'

'Wow, okay.' I took a moment to digest this. It wasn't something I had come across before, a patient's relative taking their medication as they lay dying upstairs. 'Have you spoken to Mrs Price or Jack about it?'

'No, not yet. But if it's true, we would have to report it to the police,' Philippa said. 'I was going to go there today to speak with both of them, but I was rather hoping you would want to come with me and we would do it together.'

Well, that sounded like I had no choice. I had to see Rosie every two weeks anyway, so this could double up as that visit.

'I could meet you after I finish my morning surgery, if that works for you?' I replied.

'Meet me outside the house, we will go in together.' Philippa hung up.

Rosie lived in a semi-detached, three-bedroom house. She had been living with her mum for nearly three months now and had been confined to her bed for the last two of them. Her bedroom was just big enough to put a double bed and chest of drawers in. There was a small TV in the corner which was constantly switched on. Her mum told me that the voices from the television comforted Rosie.

The front door opened directly into the living room. Jack let us in when we arrived, grunted a hello and disappeared into the

Chapter 14

back of the house. Philippa was right, there was definitely the smell of marijuana in the air. Mrs Price came downstairs.

'Hi, Dr Khan, hello Philippa. Sit down.' She gestured to the sofa.

'How are you, Mrs Price?' I asked.

'You know, Dr Khan ...' She left it there. The truth is, I didn't know. Unless you had looked after your dying daughter, you would never know.

'Is Rosie comfortable?' I said. Mrs Price bit her bottom lip and nodded.

'Would you like some tea?' she asked. We both declined.

'Mrs Price, we have come to talk to you about the missing medication,' Philippa said. Mrs Price nodded again. She played with her wedding ring, turning it round and around on her finger. There must have been a Mr Price at one point, but I had never asked about him. He definitely didn't live here now.

'Mrs Price, the most important thing for us is that Rosie is kept as comfortable as possible,' I said, taking over from Philippa. 'If she is in urgent need of pain medication, the nurses need to know that it is available at the home for them to administer. If it is not here, there will be delays in Rosie getting the medication, increasing the amount of time she is in pain.'

Mrs Price nodded again.

'Do you know who might have broken the lock and taken the medication?' Philippa asked. This was starting to feel more like a police interrogation than a consultation. Philippa must have thought the same, as she added, 'We just want what's best for Rosie.'

Silence.

Mrs Price looked up at the ceiling. 'It won't happen again,' she said quietly. 'I will make sure of it.'

'Thank you, Mrs Price, but we still need to know who took the medication,' Philippa said.

Mrs Price shook her head and tears welled up in her eyes. 'You just need to know it won't happen again. You can keep the medication here; it will be safe.'

Philippa looked at me and made a face that said 'say something'.

'Mrs Price, why don't you take me upstairs to see Rosie?' I said. She looked relieved for a break in the conversation and motioned for me to follow her.

Rosie was not conscious. Mrs Price sat on the edge of the bed and held her hand. 'She last opened her eyes two days ago,' she said. 'Sometimes I wonder if she is hungry. She hasn't had anything to eat for nearly two weeks. Her last drink was three days ago. Will she be thirsty?'

'The medication will make sure she can't feel any unpleasant sensations,' I said. Rosie's hair had been combed perfectly and tied into a plait. Mrs Price must have seen me looking at her hair.

'She liked it like that when she was a little girl. She still looks so young, even now.'

'She is young, Mrs Price, this is no age at all,' I said, honestly. Rosie was younger than me, it felt wrong. Mrs Price nodded.

'What will you do about the missing medication?' she asked.

'Protocol states we have to inform the police of any missing controlled drugs,' I replied. 'But they generally ask us how far we want them to take it from there.'

'How far will it go?' she said, visibly alarmed at the mention of the police.

Chapter 14

'I am not sure, Mrs Price. I would have to discuss it with the other doctors and nurses at the practice and get their opinions. We all know how well you have looked after Rosie and we can only imagine what you might be going through.' I looked at Mrs Price; she had the faint smell of cigarettes and perfume coming from her. Even though she must be frantic looking after Rosie, her hair was tied up in an immaculate bun and she had pale pink lipstick and nail polish on.

'I can promise you it won't happen again,' she repeated.

'And that might be enough. I honestly don't know,' I said.

Philippa said she would discuss the case with the palliative care consultant and I said I would give her a call after I had had time to discuss it with my colleagues.

I genuinely believed that Mrs Price would make sure no further drugs were stolen from the locked safe. Rosie was likely to die in the coming days; what good would it do to put Mrs Price through the trauma of reporting the missing drugs to the police and getting them to look into her nephew too? We didn't have any proof he had done it, but it was the elephant in the room.

I managed to speak with two of my GP colleagues when I got back to the surgery. Neither had come across a similar scenario before. We agreed that the police needed to be informed but, beyond getting a crime reference number, we shouldn't take it further. I rang Philippa to tell her our thoughts and she told me her team were in agreement too. She would call the police and let me know if there was anything else I could do. I felt a wave of relief wash over me – I didn't fancy telling Mrs Price we would be pressing charges. Now I had the mammoth task of documenting everything.

At 6.30 p.m. there was a knock on my door.

'Is my chariot ready?' It was Alison. I looked at her blankly. 'You're taking me home, remember?'

'Oh yes, I'll just finish doing my referrals and we'll get off,' I said. Alison took a seat.

'What are you having for your dinner tonight?' she asked. Alison was constantly on a diet and as a result was obsessed with what everyone else was eating.

'I haven't quite decided yet. I have some vegetable lasagne left over from yesterday so I will probably eat that,' I said, happy for the normality of the question.

'I'll have a salad, but I'll have to make something more substantial for Marcus,' Alison said. 'And I have to walk the dogs when I get home, you don't fancy joining me, do you?'

I finished off my last referral letter and shut my computer down. A walk in the woods sounded just about perfect after today, but I had already agreed to meet up with Daniel.

'It sounds like fun, Alison, but I'm meeting up with Daniel tonight.'

'Ah, your friend from York? How is he doing?'

'He's OK, I think – I'm looking forward to seeing him.' To be honest, I didn't really know how he was as I hadn't caught up with him for a while. It would be good to hear how he was getting on.

Daniel and I met in a coffee shop that evening – I generally tried to avoid meeting anywhere that served alcohol as his drinking had noticeably increased since that terrible incident five years ago. There had been a coroner's inquest into the death of the little boy Daniel had seen. The family were present throughout. Daniel had told me the coroner had found there was not enough evidence for a pneumonia diagnosis when the child had initially presented to him. In the end, his defence union had come to a settlement arrangement with the family.

Although I had supported Daniel throughout all of this, it was not easy to forget there was a bereft family in the centre of this story. Young parents who had gone through the tragedy of losing their little boy and then had to re-live it all in a coroner's court. It was tragic.

Daniel went back to work after the inquest was over. It was difficult. All his colleagues went to great lengths to avoid mentioning his time off, which made him feel awkward. And it was clear he had lost confidence in his own abilities as a doctor. We talked about it occasionally but he didn't open up much. He just seemed to be soldiering on. As we sat down and ordered coffee and cakes, I asked him how he was doing.

'Oh, you know …' he said, his eyes not meeting mine.

'No, tell me,' I said. I was determined to make him open up to me this time.

He sighed heavily. 'That whole incident with inquest …'

'Yes?'

'I don't know. It has just made me take stock, Amir,' he said.

'How so?'

'I'm not sure I can work full time as a GP any more. I am not blaming anyone for what happened, but the stress of each clinic every single day, it's a wonder we don't make more mistakes,' he said.

'Yes, it can feel that way,' I said. 'I'm just glad you're washing your hair these days.'

'Get lost,' he said, smiling.

It was good to see him smile, but I could still see the strain in his face. We talked it over and I tried to reassure him that what he was feeling was normal and that he was good at his job. I'm not sure I persuaded him. We parted ways, full of lemon drizzle cake, and promised to meet up again sooner next time. We always said that but it never seemed to happen.

Afterwards, I found myself thinking about what he had said. Being a doctor was a high-pressured job that came with huge responsibilities. But surely we knew that when we applied? The problem was every day new things were being added to the role of being a GP and nothing was being deducted, leaving for a very unhealthy workload. I thought of some of the cases I had seen that day, ranging from the absurdity of Mr Butler to the tragedy of Rosie Price. There weren't many jobs that would take in such a wide spectrum of human life on one day. It meant that we were constantly on our toes, trying to make life-or-death decisions under enormous pressure, never knowing if the symptoms we were being presented with were caused by a simple virus or a deadly, life-threatening disease. Or, indeed, whether a hammer was just a tool to help tether a horse or a potentially lethal weapon.

Chapter Fifteen

People have many different reasons for wanting to avoid going into hospital. Some fear being uprooted from the familiar surroundings of home; some worry about picking up an infection in a crowded ward; others simply find the antiseptic smell, the beeping machines and the proximity to suffering overwhelming and frightening. Let's face it, none of us would choose to go into hospital if we could avoid it. But for some people there was a specific fear that could create a very real problem if a hospital stay was unavoidable. I was reminded of this one day when I saw two very different patients who, for their own reasons, had an entrenched resistance to hospital admission.

There are laws that govern all home visits, nobody tells you about them but they exist. Talk to any healthcare professional who sees housebound patients at home and they will verify them. Currently I was being plagued by the first law:

'If you are looking for number 23 St Helen's Court, you will find numbers 21 and 25, but the whereabouts of 23 will remain a mystery until you have driven up and down the same street several times, being watched by several curtain twitchers (who assume you are kerb crawling).'

I wasn't happy. I had already fallen foul of the other law of home visits on a previous patient that day: 'Thou will have to wait at least fifteen minutes outside a nursing home before any of the staff deem you important enough to buzz in.' I had waited seventeen minutes to be exact, and in the end I had had to call reception and tell them I had been pressing the buzzer and it was pouring with rain outside and could they please let me in to see the patient they had asked me to assess. The polite receptionist had apologised and told me they had all been in a meeting.

I drove past number 21 St Helen's Court again; perhaps number 23 was down a hidden alleyway I hadn't seen yet? No, no alleyway. I tried ringing the patient to get directions but there was no answer. My satnav kept telling me I had arrived at my destination. I turned her off.

I looked at number 21 and then at number 25. Surely I was missing something glaringly obvious? Perhaps it was like in the Harry Potter books where I had to say a magic spell and the two houses would pull apart revealing house number 23. *That would be pretty cool*, I thought.

I had to get this visit done and get back for my afternoon clinic; I needed to get this show on the road. No time for idle magical thoughts.

There was an elderly lady standing inside a bus shelter a few yards ahead. I pulled up and wound down the window.

'Excuse me, do you know where number 23 is?'

It was still raining, and the lady was wearing a raincoat and a plastic rain bonnet on her head which reminded me of the Queen. The woman immediately opened the passenger door to my car and got in.

'Thank you, I've been waiting at that bus stop for nearly half an hour, you're a saint,' she said, buckling her seatbelt.

I stared at her, too shocked to say anything.

Chapter 15

'Are you okay, love?' she asked, as if I was the one behaving strangely.

'Can I help you?' I said, leaning as far away as possible from the intruder.

'Yes, thank you. If you could take me to town that would be lovely. I must have missed my bus, and I wanted to be home before dark.' She was looking comfortable now. 'Does this car have heated seats? My son's does, they are lovely at this time of year.'

I nodded and switched on her heated seat. I started to wonder whether St Helen's Court really was a magical road where houses appeared out of nowhere and little old ladies just got into stranger's cars. I did a quick risk assessment in my head: this lady had to be at least seventy, the chances of her attacking or raping me were pretty slim and I couldn't really send her back out in the rain now I had switched on her heated seat.

'Whereabouts in town?' I asked.

'If you could drop me off at Debenhams, that would be perfect,' she replied.

I started the engine and off we went.

'I was looking for number 23, but couldn't find it,' I said again to the lady.

'Nobody ever can, you have to go into the front garden of number 25, and it's down some stairs at the front of the house.'

'Thank you,' I said.

'Are you a doctor?' the lady asked. She must have seen me startle. 'Your stethoscope is poking out of the top of your bag,' she said, gesturing to the back seat.

'Yes I am, a GP.'

'I can never get an appointment with my doctor. I think I would have to be dying before they would see me,' she said. 'Lucky, I'm as fit as a 25-year-old.'

'Trust me, we are not sitting around doing nothing. If you can't get an appointment, it's because we are seeing lots of other people.'

'Oh I know, I can imagine how busy you are. Just here is fine,' she said as we pulled up outside Debenhams. She opened the door and got out. 'Don't forget, go into number 25 and down the steps at the front.' She closed the door and trundled off.

The mystery lady had been right: number 23 was in the basement of 25. I knocked on the door.

Audrey Guler was forty-two years old and lived alone. When I had seen her age, I was surprised we had approved a home visit for her. These were normally reserved for patients who were elderly or palliative, but reading through her notes I could see she suffered from multiple sclerosis and could only mobilise with a wheelchair. Multiple sclerosis was one of those particularly cruel conditions that struck perfectly fit and well people seemingly at random and after a period of crippling fatigue, pain and weakness would leave you paralysed and open to all sorts of infections.

This is what I had come to see Audrey for today, as she had reported feeling short of breath.

I followed Audrey into her living room. The whole house had been adapted for wheelchair living.

'Would you like a cup of tea?' Audrey asked. Her multiple sclerosis had reduced her voice to a whisper, which made me strain to hear her.

'No thank you, I get plenty of tea and coffee at the practice, probably more than I need,' I replied. 'Tell me about your breathing.'

'It has just come on over the last day or so. I haven't had a cough or a fever. Normally I would know when I am coming down with a chest infection and need antibiotics.' She lifted herself out of her wheelchair using her arms and pulled herself into an armchair.

'Do you smoke?' I asked.

'No, never.'

'Any chest pain?'

'Occasionally when I take a deep breath.' To prove it she took a deep breath and pressed on her right lower rib cage. 'It hurts just here.'

I nodded. 'Do you mind if I have a listen to your chest?' It was Audrey's turn to nod.

Audrey's chest was clear but her breathing was laboured. I pressed on her ribcage to see if I could induce some of the pain she was having, but I couldn't. I took out my oxygen saturation probe and placed it on Audrey's index finger. It flashed briefly as it picked up a signal then read 88 per cent. This was bad. Most people who had healthy lungs have oxygen saturations of 96 per cent and above, and even those who have knackered their lungs through smoking have saturations around the 92 per cent mark. Something had happened to Audrey's lungs to prevent them oxygenating her blood as they should.

'Could I have a look at your legs, Audrey?' I asked. I had a hunch.

'You will have to pull up my pyjama bottoms yourself, I can't.'

I looked at Audrey's lower leg; the left one looked considerably more swollen than the right. I asked her if she had noticed this herself.

'To be honest, I have had very little sensation in my legs for years now. I wouldn't notice if one was more swollen than the other.'

Fair enough, I thought.

'Audrey, I think you may have a clot on your leg, a DVT, and I am worried that part of this clot has broken off and travelled to your lungs.' I paused, giving her time to take it in. Doctors use a method called 'chunk and check' when giving information. We give medical information in bite-size chunks, allowing patients time to digest them before moving on to the next piece of information. 'It is something called a pulmonary embolus and can give you chest pain and shortness of breath.'

'Has it got something to do with my MS?' Audrey asked.

'Maybe. People who are less mobile are prone to DVTs so it could be a contributing factor.'

'How do we treat it?'

'We will have to diagnose it first. Because it can be a potentially life-threatening condition, we need to get you into hospital for a scan and some blood-thinning medication.'

Audrey didn't say anything.

'Audrey?'

'I am not going into hospital,' Audrey said flatly.

'Audrey, I know hospital can be a difficult place when you have physical needs, but I will make them fully aware of yours and I won't send you to the A & E department, we'll get you admitted onto a ward,' I said, trying to second-guess her.

'Dr Khan, I appreciate your advice, but I am not going into hospital.'

This wasn't going well. Audrey had every right to decline a hospital admission, but a pulmonary embolus could kill her. I could potentially start some blood thinner medication on her at home, but couldn't be sure of the diagnosis until she had had a CT scan of her chest.

Chapter 15

'Audrey, do you mind me asking you why you don't want to be in hospital?'

'I'm not leaving my cat,' Audrey said. 'I know you'll say it is a silly reason, but he is important to me and I can't leave him on his own.' Audrey pointed to the corner of the room where a rather rotund cat was curled up on a cushion. Why hadn't I noticed him until now?

'I don't think it's a silly reason,' I said. It wasn't the first time a patient had refused to leave their pet behind. 'Do you have someone who could pop in and feed him once a day while you are in hospital?'

'No, I'm not leaving him here on his own all that time. He'll be lonely. He'd have to go and stay with someone.'

'Well, do you have any family who could take him?'

'My mum lives in Birmingham and I don't have any other family.'

'Friends?'

She shook her head.

I thought hard. There must be a solution to this problem. 'Do you want me to see if there are any local catteries that might take him in short term?'

'I'm not leaving him in a cattery. He's frightened of other cats, he'll be scared.'

'What about number 25, upstairs? Are you on friendly terms with them?'

Audrey opened her mouth to say something, then closed it again.

'Audrey, listen to me. If this is a pulmonary embolus, then it could potentially kill you. Then who would be around to look after ...'

'Jacob,' she said.

'Jacob,' I continued. 'Surely he's better off spending a couple of days upstairs than being put in a cat shelter if the worst was to happen?'

Audrey sighed. 'I suppose I could ask Katrina upstairs if she could look after him. It'll only be for a couple of days, won't it?'

'Most probably,' I said vaguely.

I left Audrey with a letter to give to the ward staff. She refused a 999 ambulance so we compromised and arranged for an ambulance to pick her up in a couple of hours, after she had arranged for her neighbour to feed the cat. I drove back to the surgery. I understood how important pets were to people and how in a world where a chronic disease could isolate you from family and friends, animals could provide much-needed companionship and loyalty.

The rain had stopped by the time I got back to the surgery. I hurried into reception.

'Tamara, I have just been to visit Audrey Guler,' I said to our receptionist. 'She needs an ambulance arranging to take her to ward 31 at the hospital but she will ring to let us know when she is ready, just as soon as she has sorted out care for Jacob.'

Tamara was writing down everything I said on a pad of paper. 'Is Jacob her child?'

'No, her cat.'

Tamara wrote down 'cat' on her pad and underlined it twice. 'Got it.'

My first patient that afternoon was Mr Bostock, a 78-year-old regular at the surgery. He pushed in his shopping trolley as he entered and set it carefully aside. He spent the first three minutes of our ten-minute consultation meticulously taking off

Chapter 15

several layers of clothing, folding them and placing them on the empty chair next to him.

'It's cold outside,' he said. 'You need layers.'

'So you do, Mr Bostock. How can I help?'

'I have had a letter from the hospital, I have to go in for some tests,' he said. 'It'll all be on your computer.'

There was an assumption among a lot of people that their GP will have read the entirety of their medical records before calling them to their room. The reality is that with each patient booked in at ten-minute intervals, with no gaps in between each one, we generally skim through the last consultation on the record and hope that will tell us everything we need to know.

'Tell me about the tests you're having,' I said, carefully avoiding saying I hadn't had time to look through his records.

'Well, I saw Dr Towers last week and told her I was bleeding from my back passage, and she said I needed to be referred to see a specialist at the hospital to rule out cancer. Well, at my age, I guess you always need to rule it out.'

He was trying to make light of it, but I have yet to meet a patient wasn't worried about bleeding and not having cancer.

'Are you still bleeding from your back passage?'

'No, it seems to have stopped now.'

'Have you had any thoughts yourself as to what it might be?'

'I thought it was piles at first, that's another thing you get at my age. But Dr Towers said we needed to be sure. Anyway, they want me to have a camera shoved up my bum. That's what the letter says.' He pulled the letter from his pocket and placed it on the table.

'Yes, they usually do when we refer people with these symptoms,' I said, making a show of reading the letter, although it didn't have any useful information on it.

'Well, they want to keep me in overnight, something to do with the medication I am on.'

Mr Bostock was on a whole range of medication, from inhalers to blood thinners. He was at high risk of bleeding from the procedure so was probably being kept in as a precaution.

Mr Bostock started to well up.

'Mr Bostock, is everything okay?' I said. His tears had caught me by surprise.

'I really don't want to be kept in overnight,' he said quietly. I handed him a tissue and he wiped his eyes. The small joints in his fingers were swollen from arthritis and his hand was peppered with age spots. He suddenly looked very old and vulnerable.

I put my hand on his. 'Tell me why.'

'The ward they want to keep me on, that's where Walter, my friend, died. I couldn't face going back there.' He smoothed his trousers. 'I am willing to pay to go privately so I don't have to go to that ward.'

I looked at Mr Bostock. I had met him several times over the years and knew that Walter had been more than just a friend. In fact, they had lived together. Walter was diagnosed with bowel cancer, which spread to his bones and lungs. Mr Bostock had wanted him to die at home, but in the end he had been admitted to hospital because a doctor who didn't know him had been called out to the house in the middle of the night, diagnosed him with pneumonia and called an ambulance. He had died two days later in hospital, in a strange place being looked after by strangers. We should have done better. I would do better this time.

'Don't worry, Mr Bostock, you won't have to pay to get this done. Would it be helpful if I rang the hospital and got you moved to another ward?'

Chapter 15

'I don't mind having tests done, but I don't want to stay over-night at the hospital.' Mr Bostock was crying again. 'Last time I was there they couldn't get me on an all-male ward, so I spent the night on a mixed-sex ward. There was a man taking drugs on one side of me and two people making love on the other side.'

I wasn't expecting that. It was true the hospitals were under-funded and understaffed (through no fault of their own) and at times I had found it difficult finding a bed when I had to admit some very sick patients. But Mr Bostock's experience sounded particularly bad.

'Why don't I ring the consultant's secretary and see if I can get your colonoscopy done as a day case instead?' I said. It was the only option left.

'Do you think it will be possible?' Mr Bostock looked hopeful.

'Well, we'll never know unless we ask,' I said. It didn't sound impossible, I just had to talk to the right people.

'I really don't mind paying, if I have to,' he repeated.

'Leave it with me, Mr Bostock, I'll ring the hospital and see what I can do. Why don't I phone you with the outcome this evening?'

'Dr Khan, I would be so grateful. I don't want to be a nuis-ance, but I just couldn't face going in overnight.'

'Leave it with me.'

I watched as he unfolded his two cardigans and coat and fas-tened up every button. I promised to ring him before I went home.

I rang the hospital after seeing my next two patients. It was fairly straightforward, and the consultant I spoke with was very helpful. She said she would move Mr Bostock to the top of the morning list, keep an eye on him for the rest of the day, and let him go home in the evening, all being well.

I was about to ring Mr Bostock and tell him the good news when Tamara knocked on the door.

'Amir, there is a bit of an issue with Audrey Guler,' she said, clutching her notepad.

'What kind of issue?'

Tamara looked down at her pad as if she was reading the next part. 'Well, turns out the neighbour's granddaughter is allergic to cats, so she can't have Jacob stay in their flat.' She looked up again. 'So Audrey says she no longer wants to go to hospital.'

Shit.

I stared at Tamara who was looking back at me.

'Is there anyone else who can look after the cat?' I asked.

Tamara looked down at her pad, then at me and shrugged. 'She sounded certain she wasn't going into hospital.'

'Thanks, Tamara, I'll ring her.' Tamara looked relieved and left.

I am all about patient choice and have had many discussions with patients about what their preferred treatment options are. I understand perfectly well that patients are capable of making decisions about their own health and, whether or not I agree with them, I have to respect them. The most common scenario usually involves elderly people, like Mr Bostock, who have legitimate reasons for not wanting to go to hospital, or very sick people for whom hospital isn't appropriate. I have even had patients who otherwise had a great quality of life refuse hospital admission because they were adamant they wanted treating at home despite the risks, and that was fine. It was their choice. But I wasn't about to let a young lady die because there was nobody to look after her cat.

I dialled Audrey's number. No answer. It was the same when I tried again. I went back into reception and asked Tamara to keep ringing her while I got on with my clinic.

Chapter 15

At 6 p.m. I was getting anxious that we hadn't managed to get hold of Audrey. Either she had dropped dead from her pulmonary embolus and was lying on the floor of her apartment while Jacob looked on, or she knew it was us trying to call her and she didn't fancy being talked into going to hospital.

'Do you want me to do anything else?' Tamara asked.

'No, I'll pop in on my way home and have one last go at convincing her,' I said. *Or calling the coroner to report a death*, I thought. 'Thanks for trying though, Tamara.'

It was dark now but thankfully I knew exactly where number 23 was.

I knocked. I could see the living room light was switched on but couldn't see any movement. I knocked again, no answer.

Most GPs have been in this rather precarious situation, when you suspect that a patient you have come to visit might be dead, injured or incapacitated and cannot get to the door or call for help. Usually the patient has just been on the toilet and is late getting to the door. Occasionally the patient isn't as housebound as they let on and have gone to have their hair done. But every so often, your hunch is right. I was hoping this wasn't one of those times.

I opened up the letter box and called through, 'Audrey, it's Dr Khan. Are you there?' No answer.

The right thing to do in these situations is to call the police to get a welfare check done. If they can't get the patient to answer the door they break it down using a battering ram. It is all very dramatic. You can be left with egg on your face when the patient appears from another room, perfectly fine, wondering what on earth is going on. To make matters worse, it is on the patient to get their door fixed (which, understandably, they are never happy about). It had happened to me once before when I was a GP trainee and the patient had been out. When he came home he wasn't very happy about his door. The police left me to deal with it and I ended up paying him for the costs of his broken door myself.

I was about to get out my phone and make the call when I saw movement through the frosted glass of the front door. I breathed a sigh of relief as Audrey opened the door.

'Dr Khan, it takes me some time to get into my wheelchair and to the front door,' she said. Audrey looked visibly short of breath now.

'Sorry, Audrey,' I said, feeling foolish. 'I thought something had happened to you.' She turned her wheelchair around and I followed her in.

'I told your receptionist I wasn't going into hospital, so if you are here to convince me otherwise you are wasting your breath.' Audrey's breathing was definitely more laboured and it may have been the lighting, but she looked pale too.

'I came to see if you were okay. You weren't answering your phone,' I said. I was slightly irked; it was way past my home time and I wasn't getting any recognition of that from Audrey. She didn't say anything. 'And I came to make sure that the only reason you didn't want to go to hospital was because of Jacob.'

'I know you think it's a silly reason, Dr Khan, but to me he is family.'

'I don't think it is a silly reason, Audrey, but I also don't think it is worth dying for.'

Audrey didn't say anything again. We were stuck.

I knew what I had to do. I didn't want to say it but I was worried that if Audrey didn't get the treatment she needed she wouldn't last until morning.

'Audrey, if you agree to go to hospital, I will look after Jacob for you.' There, I had said it.

Chapter 15

'Really?' Audrey looked just as surprised as I must have. 'He is litter-trained.'

'Yes,' I said, sighing. 'I grew up having a cat, it won't be too difficult.'

'He is an indoor cat, you mustn't let him outside,' she said. 'He might get kidnapped.'

'I'll take good care of him. Now let me call that ambulance.'

Audrey gave me a strict list of cat instructions, two days' worth of cat food and treats, a litter tray and a scratching pole. She hugged and kissed Jacob in the way only pet owners can and placed him carefully into his carry case. I waited for the ambulance to arrive before packing him into my car and driving home.

I phoned my mum, who was a cat expert, for advice. I told her about Jacob.

'I would have him here in a flash but you know Jess doesn't like other cats in the house,' Mum said. Jess was my mum's cat, or princess to be exact. Mum had once tried to introduce another cat, Ruby, into the household and three days of hissing and spitting ensued. It was like a scene from Pet Cemetery. She decided after that time that Jess was a lady of solitude. Poor Ruby was adopted by my sister instead.

'I know, Mum, it should be easy. Cats basically look after themselves, right?'

'That's what all non-cat owners say,' she replied. 'It's not just feeding them, Amir, they like to be talked to and petted too.'

Jacob was mewling in the back seat. He clearly didn't like his new minder.

'Before I forget,' my mum continued. 'Aunty Zara had a fall in the garden earlier today. She says she is fine but I told her you would come and check her over on your way home.'

Mum had a way of doing this, promising my services to other people. Aunty Zara wasn't a real 'aunty'; in fact, we weren't related at all. She was a friend of my mum's, but we call anyone who is around the same age as my parents aunty and uncle.

In fact, I sometimes call my elderly South Asian patients 'Aunty' or 'Uncle' instead of 'Mr' or 'Mrs'. It feels more culturally appropriate and puts them at ease. A medical student who was sitting in clinic with me once asked if I was related to all my patients. I laughed, not realising what it might sound like to someone not from that culture.

'Mum, it's been a long day and I have a cat in the back of my car,' I said.

'It will only take you a few minutes,' Mum replied.

There was no point arguing, the die had been cast. Aunty Zara was expecting a house call and it was on my way home.

'Fine,' I said, hanging up.

I left Jacob in the car while I checked on Aunty Zara. Mum was right; she had only sustained a slight graze to her lower back. She gave me a parcel full of pakoras and samosas by way of a thank you, which I took gratefully, not wanting to cook tonight.

Jacob ran straight under the sofa when we got home. I tried to coax him out with some treats but he was having none of it. I filled up his litter tray and put fresh water in his bowl and went upstairs.

While in the shower I suddenly realised I hadn't called Mr Bostock back about his colonoscopy. I thought about putting it off until tomorrow but then remembered how worried he had been about it. I logged into the work computer system from home and dialled his number. He was thrilled with the news and told me he had thought I had forgotten about him.

'It has been a very strange day, Mr Bostock,' I said. He thanked me and hung up.

Chapter 15

There was an odd smell coming from downstairs. I went to investigate.

Jacob had done a turd just to the side of his litter tray on my new wooden flooring. He then appeared to have tried to kick some of his litter tray sand on top of the turd in an effort to cover it, leaving my entire hallway covered in cat litter. Jacob was sitting in the corner of the hallway watching me defiantly.

Great, I thought. This was going to be a long couple of days.

Audrey did turn out to have a pulmonary embolus which was treated successfully with blood-thinning injections and tablets. I was able to return Jacob to her after four long days. I wish I could say that he only soiled my floor the one time, but that would be a lie. Jacob seemed to have a habit of emptying his bowels just to the side of his litter tray. I am pretty sure he did it deliberately in an effort to piss me off enough that I would deliver him back to his mum.

For weeks following Jacob's departure I was like Lady Macbeth, constantly scrubbing the same spot, but no matter how hard I tried there remained the faint aroma of cat poo. Perhaps the smell had lodged itself into the back of my nose as nobody else seemed to notice it was there.

I got a card from Mr Bostock two weeks later, thanking me for the efforts I had made to keep him out of hospital. He told me the consultant had found only internal haemorrhoids on the colonoscopy and he had to up his fibre intake. I have a folder in which I keep all my thank-you cards. Getting thank-you chocolates and little gifts is a lovely part of being a GP, but nothing is nicer than a handwritten card. One day, when I am having a particularly bad day, I will sit down and read them all.

Chapter Sixteen

In March 2020, everything changed.

Earlier in the year there had been news stories of a new virus emerging in Wuhan, China. A respiratory virus had appeared that was killing a significant number of the people it infected. There were images of a patients looking terribly unwell in intensive care in hospitals and of citizens confined to their homes. As disturbing as the pictures were, it seemed a million miles away. Watching them, I felt like I always do when I see a disaster unfurl on another continent: *Those poor people, it must be awful for them. Thank goodness it isn't happening here.*

It was sad and worrying, but it felt detached from life in the UK.

As the weeks went on, the virus, now known as the coronavirus or Covid-19, edged closer to the UK. Italy was hit first: similar images came out of their news outlets, hospitals were overwhelmed and there was an increasing number of fatalities. The story dominated the news. Nobody was talking about anything else. It no longer felt a million miles away; it suddenly felt close.

I came home from work one evening in early March. It had been a busy day and I had been on call. A patient had called just as I was leaving complaining of severe abdominal pain and he insisted on being seen, telling us he would go to A&E if we didn't see him that evening. It turned out he was just constipated but it had kept me and my poor receptionist back an extra hour as we waited for him to arrive. My mum had called me on my way home to tell me she was making one of my favourite dishes: *aloo paratha*. These are soft chapattis that are filled with potato and spices and then covered in butter and cooked in a frying pan. Basically, they are heart disease on a plate but they taste delicious, and after the day I'd had it was exactly what I needed (and I didn't want to upset my mother by refusing). I stopped by to pick some up. Looking at the mountain of *parathas* she gave me, I wondered if I was going to end up constipated tomorrow. It was a risk worth taking.

After a quick shower, I popped the *parathas* in the microwave and sat down in front of the television. The news was still reporting the rising numbers of cases of coronavirus in Italy but this report was different – they were talking about the numbers of Italian healthcare workers who had contracted the virus from their patients and had died. Colleagues of doctors and nurses who were now themselves patients in intensive care gave grim interviews about how their friends had just collapsed at work after developing a fever and cough. Another nurse talked about how one of the doctors who worked in the emergency department had died of Covid-19 the week before. I turned the volume up, leaving greasy fingerprints all over the remote control.

This was all new to me. I had dealt with infectious diseases during my time in hospital and as a GP but there was never any real danger of me contracting the disease myself. Even when I had seen children with measles, one of the most infectious diseases known to man, I was safe in the knowledge that my mother was sensible enough to get me fully vaccinated and I was now immune to it and wasn't at risk. Occasionally, I would contract a cold or tummy bug from a patient I had seen a few days previously but, apart from muttering a few choice curse words in my head, I got over it. I had even seen a case of leprosy when I was working in hospital and I had gone into the room the patient was in along with the rest of my team. The consultant spoke with the patient about the treatment and we all left, and it never crossed my mind that I would go on to develop leprosy myself. It just wouldn't happen.

Of course, I remembered hearing about the healthcare workers in Africa who had contracted Ebola during the outbreak there, but again that seemed a million miles away.

After watching the news report on the Italian healthcare workers, I recognised a strange feeling inside of me. Panic. It was a new sensation. If I got the coronavirus from one of my patients, there was a chance I could die. I went to bed but couldn't sleep. The images of doctors and nurses in ICU beds being looked after by their colleagues kept me awake. I tried to rationalise it; there had been some isolated incidents in the UK so far but it was nothing like Italy here. We would be fine. I would be fine. Sleep eventually came.

Soon after that, the emails started coming in thick and fast. Covid-19 was here. We were being told to take extra care with patients who might have returned from South-east Asia and now Italy. We had to ask everyone whether they had a fever or cough before they were allowed into the building. But we were still seeing patients as normal and, although there was a sense of unease in the air, everything carried on as it always did.

That sense of uncertainty continued over the coming days. There was now an increasing number of cases of Covid-19 affecting people in the UK and our staff were asking questions about their safety at work. We eventually had our first case in Yorkshire,

Chapter 16

which tipped the unease into serious concern over safety and prompted an emergency meeting within the partnership. Looking around the room at the ten other partners present, I imagined that this was how it must feel to be in one of the government's COBRA meetings. We were dealing with a crisis that could affect the 100-plus employees we had, we had little information and guidance to go on and, at this early stage in the pandemic, we weren't exactly sure what to do for the best. So *exactly* like a COBRA meeting.

'The staff are getting worried about the rising numbers of cases being reported locally,' Jennifer, our business manager, said. 'Up until now we've been operating a normal service, but it's clear we need to decide whether this is still appropriate.'

The virus was known to spread primarily through droplets in coughing, sneezing and to some degree breathing and talking. As well as this, people could harbour the virus and show no symptoms for up to two weeks. Some of the respiratory procedures we carried out to diagnose lung conditions were deemed high risk for spreading the virus. We decided the time had come to cease all face-to-face contact unless it was urgent. From the following day, every patient consultation would be done remotely.

I had always been a bit envious of people who could 'work from home'. I imagined it to be nothing like *real* work at all – you could leave your computer on and sneak away to put the washing on, take a stroll around the garden or clean the bathroom. In my head, it wasn't really the same as working from an office. I also thought it was impossible for GPs to work from home. How could we? We have to see patients, examine them, check their observations. None of this is possible while separating your whites from your colours and emptying the dishwasher. But now it was thrust upon us.

We put signs up on our doors: '*We are no longer allowing patients to walk in without a booked appointment. Please go home and phone the surgery first.*' We had never done this before; our doors were always open. Well, between 7 a.m. and 8 p.m. anyway.

It turned out the patients were more nervous about the coronavirus than we were. The next day, social distancing and self-isolation measures were put in place by the government. On a normal day, all of our GP appointments were usually filled by around 10 a.m. and, unless it was an urgent medical problem, patients who rang after this were told to ring back the following morning. It was now 4 p.m. and we still had empty telephone slots. Even our regulars were not calling us up.

Had they never really been that unwell in the first place or were they all sitting at home with an assortment of maladies and ailments, too afraid to go out for fear of catching the virus? We didn't know but it was concerning. Those who we did ring were quite happy to be managed on the phone or via a video consultation. They didn't want to get the virus either.

The following week we had news. GP practices across the city were being divided into zones. Patients who had symptoms of Covid-19 and needed to be seen but were not unwell enough to go to hospital were going to be assessed by GPs in what were known as Red Zones. Those who didn't exhibit symptoms but needed to be seen for other things such as abdominal pain, rashes or leg swellings could be seen in Green Zones. Our practice was a designated Green Zone but we all had to do shifts in the Red Zones.

We had heard about the increasing numbers of patients attending the local hospital with Covid-19 symptoms. This was our attempt to help our hospital colleagues and keep people out of hospital who didn't need to be there.

But it was scary.

Chapter 16

The first doctor in the UK had now died while treating patients with Covid-19. Reports of other healthcare practitioners dying in Italy and Spain were still coming through.

'How are you feeling, Amir?' Oliver asked me. Oliver was one of the other GP partners. We were sitting in one of the consulting rooms, wearing scrubs. He had brought me in a coffee and then quickly scuttled off to the far side of the room to maintain social distancing.

I stared at him. I had a Red Zone shift booked in the next day. The email had just arrived in my inbox. I felt slightly sick.

'I'm shitting it, Oli,' I said honestly. It was a strange feeling. I felt bad for being scared. My colleagues at the hospitals were seeing patients with symptoms all the time. Were they this scared? The nation as a whole had started calling healthcare workers 'angels' and 'heroes'. I certainly didn't feel like either while I was sitting there feeling this panicked about going to the Red Zone.

'Yeah, I would be too,' Oliver said, looking over my shoulder at the email. 'I haven't been allocated my shift there yet.' Oli was in his mid-fifties, and always well versed in all the latest evidence and guidelines. He was also always focused on the worst-case scenario in any situation. 'Statistically, you are more likely to die from Covid-19 being of South Asian heritage and I am in a higher risk group for being over fifty.' He took a slurp from his coffee. 'Either way, we're buggered if we get it.'

'So now I'm *really* shitting it. Thanks, Oli.' I laughed. 'I'm sure it will be fine, we just need to be careful.' I didn't feel this confident inside but someone needed to balance out Oli's perpetual state of doom.

'Let's hope they have the proper protective gear by then. There's been an issue sourcing goggles,' he said. It was true, we'd had trouble getting hold of goggles for our staff too, and in the end a local funeral director had donated twelve pairs to us and they were now safely locked away in a cupboard in reception. Even I wasn't quite sure who had the key.

'Also, if you're seeing lots of Covid-19 patients in a short period of time, you will be exposed to higher levels of the virus, which increases your risks of getting complications. It's called a high viral load.'

'Really, Oli, you're not helping. I am trying to focus on the positives,' I said, taking my first sip of coffee. It wasn't strong enough but I drank it anyway.

'What positives?' he asked.

'Well, for one, these scrubs I'm wearing are so big you can't see all the weight I've put on since I've not been able to go to the gym. I might start a campaign to keep them as our permanent work uniform after the pandemic,' I said.

Neither of us said anything for a couple of minutes.

'Have you made a will?' Oli eventually asked.

'Right, that's it. Out. I have patients to ring.' I stood up and opened the door. Oli shrugged and left.

As I drove home that night, I noticed all the rainbows that were appearing in people's windows in support for NHS workers. My fear began to turn to guilt. There was talk of 'battling' the coronavirus, of us being in a war with an invisible enemy. NHS frontline workers were the soldiers, and we had to be brave. There was no talk of us being afraid. We were all warriors. Warriors are never afraid, even in the face of death.

I had always known I would be a terrible soldier. I had read about those poor civilian men who had been drafted into the army during the world wars and knew I would have been the one whose helmet was too big or whose gun was stuck on safety. I was definitely a lover, not a fighter. But like those men, I had no choice. There was a sense of duty being drilled into us. To be honest, I was embarrassed to talk about feeling afraid. I knew that was unhealthy but everyone had done such a good job of painting us as warriors that I simply couldn't bring myself to tell anyone about how I was feeling.

On my way home, I stopped at the supermarket to get some lunch for my Red Zone shift the next day. There was nothing left on the shelves. I grabbed a packet of Pringles and some Diet Coke and left, feeling even more miserable than when I went in.

Our designated Red Zone was at a different surgery to the one I was used to working with. On my way there for my first shift, I programmed my phone to play the sounds of birdsong through my car as I drove; it usually calmed me down. Oliver tried to call me while I was en route. I ignored it.

The staff at the Red Zone consisted of two receptionists and another GP. I hadn't worked with any of them before but they all seemed reasonably relaxed about being there.

'When the patients arrive, we ask them to wait in the car park,' the receptionist said. She had told me her name when she had let me in but I hadn't quite caught it and now it was too late to ask again. She had false nails that were growing out so you could see her actual nails underneath. I suspect she usually got her nails manicured every week. *Another casualty of the lockdown*, I thought. 'I'll then go out in full PPE to fit the patient with a mask and bring them to your room,' she said. 'Tea or coffee?'

'Sorry?' I asked.

'Would you like tea or coffee?'

'Oh right, thanks,' I said.

'Well, which one will it be?' She was looking at me as if she wasn't quite sure I was a doctor.

'Tea please, just milk,' I said.

'The changing rooms are over there, scrubs in the cupboard and you can leave your things here in reception. You can't take them into the consulting room; it's a clean zone.' I frowned, looking at the corner she wanted me to leave my coat and bag in. It was just by the bins, which looked like they could overflow at any moment. 'Don't worry, nobody's going to nick them,' she said, laughing.

My first patient was already waiting in the car park by the time I logged on. I went to have a look in his notes. The keyboard and mouse were wrapped in a plastic film so they could be cleaned properly after each patient, which made it nearly impossible to type anything. It reminded me of the plastic film my dad used to put over the remote control for the television when we were kids. You had to press extra hard on the buttons to get them to work.

'It's to protect the buttons from your fingers,' he had said.

If buttons needed protection from fingers then they shouldn't be buttons, I remember thinking.

Jack was a 63-year-old man. The notes said he had a fever and was wheezy with a flare-up of his asthma. He lived with his wife who also had a fever but wasn't as unwell as him. I donned my personal protective equipment, which consisted of goggles (which they thankfully had), a surgical mask, a pair of gloves and a plastic apron. The goggles didn't quite fit and the mask didn't form any kind of seal around my face. Worse still was the flimsy plastic apron: the first one I put on tore as I knotted the ties behind my back and ended up in the bin. To be honest, the plastic covering the keyboard looked more robust than the apron. My arms, ears and large areas of my face and neck were still exposed. If this virus wanted to get me, I imagined it would have no trouble getting past this PPE. We were being told that the PPE was in keeping with national guidance and 'followed the best scientific advice' but I was yet to see any study detailing how a plastic pinny could offer any level of protection.

But soldiers don't question their generals, we just go out into battle safe in the knowledge that those in charge have done the appropriate background work to minimise the risk to our lives.

Somehow, I didn't feel that confident.

The Mystery Receptionist brought Jack into my room. She too was wearing PPE, and the patient a mask.

'This is Jack Munroe,' she said to me. 'Jack, this is Dr Khan.' She turned to leave, then spun back around. 'Oooh, I'll just take that,' she said, grabbing my empty cup and disappearing.

Even through Jack's mask I could see he was short of breath. With my normal rate of breathing, I could feel the condensation building up behind my mask. I imagined that with his increased respiratory rate the inside of Jack's was like a sauna.

GP consultations centre around building rapport with patients, allowing them to trust you before they open up about their health problems. That usually involves eye contact, warm smiles and soft questioning at the start of each consultation. Wearing PPE created a barrier between me and my patient, something I hadn't really thought about before. Jack could only see parts of my face, and I imagined that made it difficult for him to trust me, especially as this was the first time we had met. I was also required to limit my time with him to reduce the risk of infection, so any 'soft' questioning to ease us in had to be left at the door.

'Hi Mr Munroe, I'm Dr Khan. Tell me about how you are feeling,' I said, trying to convey as much warmth as I possibly could through my eyes.

'It's my breathing, doc. I have asthma but it's got pretty bad.' He took in a gasp. 'And I've got a temperature.' He put a hand to his forehead, breaking the rules about touching your face.

'How often have you been using your blue inhaler?' I asked. The blue inhaler contained a medication called salbutamol, which was only ever to be used when you felt wheezy or short of breath.

'About six times today,' he said. 'Normally, I only use it once or twice a week.'

'Okay, well, let's take a look at you,' I said, then paused.

We had been issued with instructions on what was safe to examine and what carried high risk. Rather unhelpfully, the guidance suggested keeping a metre distance from the patient where possible. Well, that certainly wouldn't work. We had also been advised not to look inside people's mouths to examine their throats as there had been a disproportionate number of ear, nose and throat specialists contracting the virus and this was thought to be due to them carrying out a large number of throat examinations.

Even more bizarrely, we had been advised to ask the patient to look in the opposite direction to you during the examination so they were not breathing on you for any significant length of time. It all felt very much against the grain.

Sometimes, it seemed as if the people who wrote 'the science' didn't understand the practicalities of seeing actual real-life patients.

'Mr Munroe, I am going to ask you to turn your head away from me while I examine you,' I said through my mask.

'You what?' Mr Munroe said, moving his head closer to me so he could hear.

'Please turn your head away from me so I can examine you,' I said, louder this time.

'Why?' Mr Munroe said, stepping closer to me.

'So you don't breathe on me,' I said, exasperated.

'Well, I've never had to do that before,' Mr Munroe said huffily, turning his head away. I could feel our rapport slipping through my fingers. I examined his chest, which sounded wheezy.

'Mr Munroe, I now need to place this oxygen probe on your finger,' I said, holding out the probe.

'What did you say?' he said, turning his head towards me again. I got a whiff of cigarettes.

'I need your finger for this probe. It's to measure your oxygen levels,' I said. I gave up on getting him to turn his head back around, it simply wasn't going to work. And besides, if I could smell the last cigarette he had smoked, I had also probably already inhaled any viruses he was breathing out.

Mr Munroe's oxygen levels were low, but not low enough to warrant hospital.

'Aren't you going to look in my throat?' he asked. 'It's been sore for the last couple of days.'

'I'm sorry, Mr Munroe, I can't,' I said, slightly embarrassed. 'Throat exams are not permitted due to the increased risk of passing on the virus.'

He narrowed his eyes. 'Well, that's bloody ridiculous.'

I issued him a prescription for some antibiotics and steroids to help with his wheeze. 'There you go,' I said, placing it on the table. 'These should help with your chest.'

'What about the test? Aren't you going to test me?' he asked, looking at the prescription.

'Test you?' I said, puzzled.

'For that China virus. I think I've got it. I've got all the symptoms.'

'I think you mean the coronavirus,' I said. 'And sorry, no, we haven't got the means to test patients for it here.'

'Well, that was a fucking waste of time then,' he said, picking up his script and getting up to go.

'You can't leave, Mr Munroe. I have to ask our receptionist to escort you out of the building,' I said, messaging the receptionist on my computer.

We both sat in an awkward silence until there was a knock on the door.

'All ready?' the Mystery Receptionist said, opening the door. Mr Munroe didn't say anything as he left, clearly disappointed in the service he had just received. I watched the door close and got up to take off my PPE. Then I went to the sink to wash my hands, singing 'Happy Birthday' out loud twice as I did so.

'Is it your birthday, love?' I jumped as the Mystery Receptionist poked her head around the door.

'Er, no. I just sing it out loud to make sure I wash my hands for twenty seconds,' I said, looking embarrassed.

'Aw, that's nice. Do you want another cup of tea? I've got some biscuits too, Bourbons. Chocolate,' she said, looking proud of herself.

'That sounds nice,' I replied. She smiled and disappeared.

Jack Munroe was right. It made all the sense in the world to test patients who came into the Red Zones for coronavirus, but currently tests were only being carried out in designated test centres and hospitals.

All the patients I saw that day had some form of fever or cough. They all managed to find a way to breathe on me. In the end I just gave up. Despite all of this, I left the Red Zone feeling better than I had when I had arrived. The Red Zone was no longer an unknown battleground and the patients were arguably

Chapter 16

more straightforward than the ones I was used to dealing with. And yes, they had the potential to pass on a deadly virus. But I was young, and the statistics said I would only get mild symptoms if I did get the infection. And, as we all know, statistics are never wrong.

My mum rang me on my way home. She was upset. One of my sisters is a consultant in the Emergency Department at the local hospital. She was dealing with patients who were very sick from the coronavirus and she was worried about bringing the virus home to her family. My mum told me she had moved out of her family home into an empty house that belonged to one of her friends, as that way she wouldn't be bringing back swathes of the virus and potentially infecting her family.

'There are lots of people off sick,' Mum said. 'So she's picking up extra shifts too, then going home to that empty house. It's just so sad.'

'It's really sad, Mum,' I said. 'But she is doing the right thing.' I imagined how miserable that must be, to deal with coronavirus patients all day and then not have the comfort of coming back to family. I knew NHS workers were doing this all over the country, but it suddenly felt more real now.

'I have made her some samosas, will you take them round for her?' Mum asked. 'I can't go; my doctor says I have to stay indoors.'

'Of course I can, Mum.' I said, turning the car around and heading towards my mum's house.

Working in the Green Zones didn't mean you couldn't come into contact with patients who might be harbouring the virus. We now had to treat every patient as though they were potentially infectious, so even when they came in with acute abdominal pain, we still wore PPE and they were still asked to look away so we could examine their tummies.

We were also still responsible for doing our own home visits to housebound patients, regardless of their symptoms. We did eventually get an email from the powers that be telling us that we should limit our visits to nursing and care home patients to emergencies only, but before that came I had been to see Mr Thornton.

Mr Thornton was eighty-three years old. He lived in one of the nursing homes our practice looked after. I had known him since he had moved into the home three years ago. He had dementia which made him muddled at times, and arthritis which meant he got about the home using a frame. The carers would cut up his food for him into bite-size pieces, but he was then able to feed himself. Mr Thornton had come to the home after an admission to hospital with a urinary tract infection; prior to that he lived at home with Mrs Thornton, his wife. It had become clear during his stay in hospital that Mrs Thornton was not able to look after him at home, and the decision was made to move him to a nursing home.

Mrs Thornton had visited him every day. She told me she got two buses to get there, but provided she left after 9.30 in the morning she didn't have to pay the bus fares.

'Senior citizens travel free after 9.30 a.m., Dr Khan,' she had said. 'There aren't many perks to getting old but that is one of them. I still wouldn't recommend it, getting old that is.'

She would stay all day, making sure he ate all of his lunch and dinner before leaving again. Since the pandemic, though, Mrs Thornton was no longer able to visit her husband. Unlike some of the other residents' family members she didn't have a phone or device that allowed her to video call her husband, and he was too

Chapter 16

confused to have any sort of meaningful conversation with her over the phone. Her days of being busy and being by her husband's side had turned to long hours confined to her home. Mr Thornton, who relied on the familiarity of his wife's face, was made to stay in his room all day along, just as all the other residents now had to stay in theirs. His meals were brought there, and he didn't even leave to go to the bathroom as he had an en suite. He hadn't left the confines of his room for nearly three weeks. Patients with dementia rely on stimulation, especially from things that remind them of their past. Without these things, their dementia worsens and they deteriorate rapidly.

That morning I got a call from the nursing home. Mr Thornton had developed a temperature the evening before; he had deteriorated overnight and his breathing had become erratic. There were two other residents at the home with similar symptoms and another GP had been out to see them the week before and sent one of them into hospital. The hospital was overwhelmed with patients who were seriously ill with the virus and had sent our care home resident back with strict instructions to isolate him from the others. The residents had already been confined to their rooms since the beginning of the outbreak, with their carers taking extra care with hygiene and cross-contamination; now they stepped up the measures still further. But with the best will in the world, we were dealing with an extraordinarily contagious virus, and inevitably it had spread.

The carers at the home needed a doctor to come out and assess Mr Thornton, as it was likely he had the same thing as many of the other residents.

To be honest, I could have diagnosed Mr Thornton with coronavirus over the phone. He had other health conditions that meant he wasn't a candidate for hospital treatment with a

241

ventilator should his condition deteriorate. The chances of him surviving anything like that were slim to none. The hospital wasn't the right place for him, and even though nobody had explicitly said it, there was an understanding that care home residents with multiple health issues were best kept at home. It felt shit, but it made sense.

I could have just advised the carers that this was likely to be the beginnings of the coronavirus and given them instructions that he be kept comfortable but isolated.

I couldn't do it. I knew Mr Thornton and I knew his wife. If I was going to manage him as a patient who was likely to be 'end of life', as it's called, the least I could do was go and see him. Plus, if I wasn't sending him to hospital, he needed a doctor to see him to make sure he wasn't suffering from something else that could be treated. Besides, the only reason I might not have gone was to protect myself from exposure to the virus, and I couldn't face saying that to his carers who were clearly still going in despite the dangers to themselves. No, I would go. It was the least I could do.

I arrived at the nursing home wearing my scrubs. I got out of the car and put on my PPE. One of the carers took to me see Mr Thornton and she waited outside while I went in.

Mr Thornton was usually sitting up in a chair, he would always say hello and then disappear back into his own world. Today he lay in bed; his eyes were closed when I went in and his breathing shallow.

'Hello, Mr Thornton,' I said gently. He opened his eyes and immediately looked frightened. I had forgotten I was wearing PPE, not something a patient with dementia wanted to see looking down at them. 'It's okay, Mr Thornton, it's Dr Khan.' He clearly didn't have the energy for any more of a reaction, so he closed his eyes and turned his head away. Well, at least he was doing that right.

Mr Thornton's oxygen levels were dangerously low, and his breathing was laboured. There was no wheeze or signs of a chest infection. This had all the hallmarks of Covid-19. I took a moment to look at him properly. The skin on the back of his hands was paper thin and the veins stood up like blue worms making their way up his arm. The top button of his pyjama top had come undone and I could see his breastbone and ribs. Normally, I would have put my hand on his arm to offer him some comfort, but the virus was so contagious it wasn't allowed.

I left the room, and spoke with the carer.

'It's probably coronavirus,' I said. 'He is so frail we can't send him to hospital. Let's try to keep him as comfortable as possible. I will organise for the appropriate medication to be delivered and will speak with the district nurses to make them aware of him, but I don't think he has much longer now.' The carer didn't ask if I was going to test Mr Thornton for the coronavirus. We both knew I hadn't been given the means with which to test him.

Instead she nodded and asked, 'Are you going to speak with his wife?'

'Yes, I'll ring her when I get back to the surgery,' I said.

I ripped off my plastic apron as I left and got into my car. It didn't feel good. Mr Thornton was now the third person in that care home to get the coronavirus and I knew there would be others. As much as I knew about how contagious the virus was and how many people were expected to die, it felt awful driving away from a care home where it was taking hold. I thought about the carer I had just spoken to and realised I hadn't even asked her what her name was. I always asked their names. Had I been so desperate to leave that I had left part of myself at the door? She must be just as worried about the virus as I was, but she was staying there. She took care of her residents.

A bird landed on the bonnet of my car, pulling me out of my thoughts. It was a robin, its red breast reflected in the metal of the car. It had something in its mouth, a piece of wool. It stared at me through the glass and then flew off to a nearby hedgerow. Almost immediately it reappeared, its beak now empty. I looked to see what it was doing but my movements startled it and it flew off. I could make out a nest inside the hedge, delicately constructed with material the robin had been collecting. The natural world was carrying on as normal. It was reassuring in a way.

I started the engine and headed back to the surgery.

When I got back, I dialled Mrs Thornton's number. Normally, I would have arranged to meet her at the nursing home or brought her into the surgery to deliver this kind of news. Face-to-face discussions were the gold standard for delivering bad news; you could pick up on the other person's body language, if tears came you could pass them a tissue and if needed you could put a hand on their hand. But things had changed.

'Hello?' Mrs Thornton said as she picked up the phone.

'Mrs Thornton, it's Dr Khan,' I said.

'Oh hello, Dr Khan, the home said you were going to phone,' she said. 'They told me Cyril was poorly.'

'He is poorly, Mrs Thornton,' I said. 'Did they tell you how poorly he was?' It was always useful to get a good idea of how much the family knew before pressing ahead.

'No, just that you would ring,' she said. 'Is he very unwell?' Her voice broke.

It is hard doing this in person. It was even harder doing it over the phone. 'Mrs Thornton, unfortunately your husband became very unwell during the night with a fever and shortness of breath. I don't think it's a run-of-the-mill chest infection.'

'It's that coronavirus, isn't it?' she said quietly.

'I think that is the most likely diagnosis,' I replied gently.

'The home phoned me earlier this week, they told me they had another resident there who had it. I knew then that Cyril would also get it.' She was sobbing now. 'People like us don't do well with this virus, do we, Dr Khan? Old people.'

'I think Cyril's age, combined with his other medical problems, does put him at higher risk,' I said.

'Will he have to go to hospital?' she asked, suddenly sounding hopeful.

'I don't think hospital is the best place for him at the moment,' I said. 'His body is too weak for the treatment there. But I promise I have done everything I can to make him as comfortable as possible.'

'"Comfortable as possible" means he is going to die,' she said, then immediately apologised. 'I'm sorry, I didn't mean to say that.'

'That's okay, Mrs Thornton,' I said. She had the right to say what she wanted.

'The worst thing is, I still can't go and see him,' she said. 'The care home said if he got really unwell I might be able to visit as it was exceptional circumstances, but my own health conditions mean I can't leave the house.' She had stopped crying now and her voice had become flat.

'I have just come back from seeing him, Mrs Thornton. The infection has made him drowsier; he really wouldn't know if you were there. You are right not to take the risk.'

'Do you think so?' she asked.

'I do,' I said.

'Will he die alone?' she asked quietly. 'I know you said he won't know if anyone is there, but I wouldn't want him to die alone.'

'I am sure the carers will be with him if his condition worsens,' I lied. Many of the carers at the home were off sick with symptoms of Covid themselves or stress. The few that were left were stretched at it was unlikely they could sit with Mr Thornton.

'That's good,' Mrs Thornton said, her voice now a whisper.

'Mrs Thornton, is there anything else I can do to help?' I asked, feeling useless.

'Do you know how long we have been married, Dr Khan?' she asked. 'Sixty-two years. Marriages don't last that long now, do they?'

I didn't say anything.

'He proposed to me at a supermarket. I was just nineteen. I mean, do you know anyone else who has been proposed to at a supermarket?' she laughed. 'He said he had meant do it at the park earlier but had lost courage.' She paused. 'He was my first boyfriend. We had only been courting three months, that was normal back then. All my friends were getting married, so I just said yes.'

'That's a pretty big gamble on three months,' I said, not really knowing what to say.

'Best thing I ever did,' she said. 'I supposed I'd better ring our son; he'll want to know. He lives in Cardiff. He hasn't been able to visit since this lockdown, and I don't know if he will be able to travel now either.'

'I think this would count as essential travel, Mrs Thornton,' I said. To be honest, I didn't know for sure, but I was aware of people travelling for much less important things.

'That's good,' she said.

Chapter 16

We said goodbye to each other and hung up. Nursing homes had it bad, they were essentially petri dishes for the virus. An ideal place for the virus to easily pick up a host, multiply and move on to the next victim. Most of the residents were not suitable for hospital treatment so couldn't be moved anywhere and those that got the coronavirus succumbed to it. These people, who had probably contributed their entire working lives to making our society a better place, were now left to fend for themselves as a virus ravaged through their home. They would spend their last few days confined to a room, isolated from the ones they loved, slowly taking their last breath. It was a terrible situation.

Mr Thornton died two days later. The home rang the surgery up and asked me to complete his death certificate.

It was the first of many calls I had to make to families of those in nursing homes. Each one broke my heart, each one shattered a family into a million pieces. I was used to having these conversations with families; what I wasn't used to was the unrelenting frequency at which I was now having them.

In between these calls I would speak to patients who were being affected by the coronavirus in other ways. Their hospital appointments had been cancelled, and treatments they had been waiting months for were now postponed 'until further notice'.

Mrs Hawkyard had been waiting fourteen months to have her right hip replaced. The surgeon had told her at her last appointment that the cartilage had worn away and now, each time she moved, exposed bone grated on exposed bone causing her excruciating pain. She told me she wasn't able to sleep at night because of the pain.

Two days before she was due to have her operation, the hospital cancelled all non-emergency surgery. She cried as she told me about the letter. I listened until she was finished and offered to increase her pain relief.

'You told me last time you couldn't do that as the medication was addictive,' she said.

She was right, but I had run out of options. The hospital had cancelled her appointment and there was no way to get her any physiotherapy.

'I know, but I am hoping it will only be temporary until we get a new date for your operation,' I said, sounding a lot more optimistic than I felt.

She had agreed to this, but we both knew it wouldn't help much.

It was one of the worst times in my career, but strangely at the same time I never felt more useful. Maybe this was that sense of duty they had been talking about. I still didn't feel like a soldier of any sort, nor did it feel like I was fighting a battle. But I did feel weary at the end of each day, more so than I had ever done before.

As the weeks went on, my anxiety around the coronavirus, Red Zones and nursing homes dissipated. The worrying novelty of seeing patients with fevers and coughs wore off and it was now part of the job. I got used to apologising to patients for their cancelled appointments and consulting in PPE.

However, no matter how comfortable I got with this new normal, it didn't stop me from feeling like I was developing a temperature and sore throat every night before I went to bed, convincing myself I had contracted the virus. Inevitably I got up the next morning feeling absolutely fine and made my way to work again.

Chapter Seventeen

There was already a message waiting me on my desk when I got into work. It was from Wendy Ashworth.

As the pandemic hit, Wendy had rung to say Emily had got a letter from the NHS stating she needed to shield. This meant they had been restricted to their home until it was safe to go outside again. Wendy's dad had been doing all their shopping for them. '*Wendy Ashworth wants you to ring her: urgent,*' the scribbled note said.

Oh God, I hoped something hadn't happened to Emily. She had had a stint in hospital not long ago with pneumonia. They had thought it was coronavirus initially, but thankfully she had tested negative. Because her lungs were already weakened, she had ended up in intensive care. They wanted to sedate her and put in a tube to help her breathe, but because of what had happened last time they decided not to. She had spent three weeks in hospital on antibiotics and oxygen. Wendy had rung me then to let me know. She hadn't been allowed to stay with Emily all the time. They had restricted her visits, due to the risk of coronavirus, and Wendy had found that especially tough.

She hadn't said it, but I think the hospital didn't expect her daughter to survive. I had rang the hospital to see if I could visit Emily, but they had initially declined. Wendy had rung them and they agreed to let me come in for a few minutes. It is not something I normally do for my patients, but I had been looking after Emily for nearly nine years and I had promised her I would always look after her.

She had lain in bed, almost unrecognisable. Her tiny body was swollen from both the collecting fluid and the steroids they were giving her to help with her breathing. She was being given two broad spectrum antibiotics through a drip in her little hand. A thin tube coming out of her nose connected to an oxygen tap in the wall. She had been asleep when I came as it was late in the evening.

Wendy had been in the parents' room at the end of the corridor. 'How is she?' I asked.

'A bit brighter today,' she'd said. 'Still not eating, but we managed to get a smile out of her.'

Emily had recovered from that pneumonia, but it had left her heart and lungs even more vulnerable. She was now in desperate need of a heart transplant. We all knew her time was running out.

She hadn't been well enough to attend school even before they had shut them down. The council had allowed her to be home schooled. A teacher had come for two hours a day and worked with her on the core subjects. Wendy had told me that when she was helping her with homework, she could almost pretend they were a normal family doing normal things. But then Emily would cough and suddenly become short of breath and she would remember that they weren't like everyone else.

It had been nearly two years since Emily had been placed on the transplant register. We all knew that finding a donor heart would be difficult, but as time went on and Emily became sicker, it felt less and less hopeful. The specialists at the hospital were

Chapter 17

worried that if she didn't get a new heart soon, her lungs would become so damaged she would need a heart and lung transplant.

Now, a few weeks after I'd made that hospital visit, I dialled Wendy's number. There was no answer, so I left a message saying I had called. I tried again after my first few patients but this time it went straight to voicemail. I had already prepared myself for the worst. Emily's condition was such now that even a simple infection could kill her.

After my morning surgery, I dialled Wendy's number again. It rang.

I was getting ready to leave another voicemail when she answered.

'Hello?' she said.

Whenever we dialled out from our surgery it appeared as a blocked number on mobile phones. Wendy didn't know it was me calling.

'Wendy, it's Dr Khan. I got your message and I'm returning your call.' I braced myself.

'Oh, Dr Khan. We got the call early this morning, they have a heart for Emily! We are at Great Ormond Street Hospital now. Emily is getting ready for theatre.' Wendy was talking in whispers; I assumed she was on the ward.

'That's great news!' I said, also in a whisper. 'Have they said how long the operation might last?' I didn't know why I was whispering – it was just in response to her whisper.

'Up to seven hours,' she replied. 'I have to go, there are some more doctors here to see us.'

'Okay, I'll try you later,' I said before hanging up.

It was good news, I thought. It was Emily's best chance. I knew the procedure came with grave risks and that long-term survival rates were not as high as you would expect, but without it Emily would be dead in a few months. I let out a breath. I felt tense.

I still had other patients to see, so I called my next one in.

I tried calling Wendy at the end of the day but it went straight to voicemail. She would have other things on her mind, I knew, so I decided to leave it until tomorrow.

Besides, I was meeting up with Daniel tonight. That would keep my mind occupied – he had said he had some big news. I was just glad to take my thoughts off Emily for the evening, as I couldn't help but worry about her. We were going for a walk along the canal.

I hadn't seen Daniel for a while – with everything going on, I hadn't even had the time to phone him. I guess, as practising GPs, we had a pretty good excuse when it came to being busy, but it was just an excuse. I knew he still had mixed feelings about his job and had done ever since he had faced that formal complaint. Nevertheless, that was now six or seven years ago and as far as I was concerned things were pretty much back to normal with him. Nothing could have prepared me for what he said as we made our way along the canal path.

'I've resigned from being a GP!' Daniel announced.

'What?' I said. I was completely stunned.

'I handed in my notice. I no longer want to be a GP,' Daniel repeated.

'Daniel, what are you talking about?' I was sure I hadn't heard him right. 'You've *resigned*?'

'I've been thinking about it for a while now. I've never been happy about going back to work since that awful incident all those years ago. I've tried, but I can't do the job like I used to, so I've quit.'

Daniel wasn't talking in a bullish way. He seemed to have come to terms with his decision and appeared now to be stating a fact.

'Wow. What will you do instead?' I asked. I often wondered what I would do if I wasn't a GP.

'I'm not sure yet, but we have some money saved up so there isn't a rush. Besides, my notice period is six months so I have plenty of time to decide. I think I might become a lawyer. I have always wanted to shout *"Objection, Your Honour!"* loudly in a court room,' he said with a smirk.

'I have a feeling you may be disappointed, if that is your main motivation for wanting to be a lawyer.'

I let his news sink in for a few minutes. I didn't know how I felt about it. I found it all rather unsettling.

'What about you?' he asked me.

'What about me?'

'Do you think you could do this job forever?'

'I'd like to think so,' I said. I hadn't stopped to think about it before. I assumed I would be a GP forever. I didn't think I had much choice. I still enjoyed the job and I hoped the patients still got something out of coming to see me.

'Don't let it wear you down, Amir,' he said cryptically.

I laughed. 'Daniel, you sound like an old man. I'll be fine.'

As the evening turned cooler, I found myself telling Daniel about Emily's operation, which was still preying heavily on my mind. She would still be in surgery right now. As we watched the cygnets follow their mum happily in the water, my mind kept drifting to Wendy and what she must be going through at that moment. How brave that family had been. How much had they endured.

It was this, I realised, that kept me in my profession. It was people like Emily and her mum.

I rang Wendy as soon as I got into work the next day. The operation had lasted a little over six hours but had gone well. Emily was in the intensive care unit and a machine was helping her heart and lungs to work, but the surgeons were optimistic. She was to stay in ITU for a week before she could be moved to another ward.

It would be nearly two weeks before Emily was transferred back to the local hospital. Her new heart was beating for itself, and although she still had some pain from the surgery this was controlled with medication. She was on a whole new list of medication to help her heart but also to prevent her body from rejecting it. That or an overwhelming infection were still very much major concerns.

Wendy told me Emily's dad had been visiting regularly. He had come down to London too and they had taken it in turns to stay with her. The hospital had an attached building with en suite bedrooms where she could get some rest when he was with Emily.

It would be two months before Emily was well enough to come to the surgery.

She wasn't poorly when she came – she came to drop off a card and chocolates for the staff. Everyone kept their distance but still managed to make a fuss of her when she came in. Almost all the staff had had some dealings with her over the last twelve years. The nurses came out and Alison was there, as well as a lot of the GPs. Emily looked a bit overwhelmed but kept smiling.

Wendy thanked everyone quietly as Emily gave the box of chocolates to Annabelle on reception. I went over to them.

'How's your new heart?' I asked her.

Chapter 17

'Good,' Emily said. 'How's Blitzen?'

'Getting ready for Christmas,' I said. She laughed.

I knew Emily wasn't out of the woods yet. She was still seeing a physiotherapist about strengthening exercises for her heart. She still had to go to frequent hospital appointments, have scans and have her bloods checked. And she was still at risk of sepsis and we were to keep a close eye on her. But here she was in reception with her new heart.

Despite her many health problems, she was surviving. She had got a new heart and was ready to start her new life.

I often think about Emily's story when I hear people complain about the NHS or having to wait to be seen. I think about the coordination of care that is required throughout multiple organisations to keep one little girl alive. The times when consultants would travel up to regional hospitals to provide expertise that would otherwise not be available in that area. The support in place for families who are going through the trauma of having a child with a life-limiting illness. Families who are kind enough to donate an organ of their deceased loved one. The part every single member of the NHS team plays to help one person.

I wonder about how marvellous it is that Emily got a second chance at life without her family having the anxiety of medical bills and the worry of mounting costs she may have faced in other countries.

When my mind goes to those dark places, recalling Mr Thornton and countless others like him who died from the coronavirus, and my brave colleagues who lost their lives treating patients with the disease, I think of Emily and her new little heart.

It can be hard working in the NHS in the current climate, but when it gets really bad I think of Emily and her new heart. And that thought keeps me going.

Epilogue

My profession is in crisis. Whenever I pick up a newspaper, switch on the news or speak to any of my colleagues, it's always the same: there are simply not enough GPs. The politicians are offering thousands more GPs in an inconceivable amount of time, and meanwhile other healthcare professionals are being drafted in to plug the gaps (this is not necessarily a bad thing). True, the profession needs an overhaul but what about those of us currently working within it? What does it do to our morale seeing these articles, listening to these stories and hearing these empty promises? We still have to go to work every single day and apologise to each patient when they complain about how difficult it is to get an appointment. That constant feeling of being on the back foot and firefighting each day has a grinding effect on our ability to switch on, smile and do the best for our patients.

But that is all we want, to do the best for our patients.

The general practitioner or family doctor has been a cornerstone of people's lives for hundreds of years. They have been the first port of call for many a sick soul.

A century ago, GPs were working as private physicians seeing patients in clinic or in their own homes, delivering babies and performing surgery – in return for a payment. Then the NHS came about in 1948 and (quite rightly) everybody was allowed access to their GP, delivered free at the point of use. It was thought that over time the initial jump in demand for general practitioners' services would gradually fall and stabilise. That never happened.

The workload in general practice continues to increase. Patients are living longer and their needs inevitably become more complex as they age. Other services within the NHS and social care are also stretched, meaning patients are waiting longer for treatments at hospitals and are not getting the support they need in the community and at home. As a result, often the only real accessible place they can turn up at for help is their GP practice. It is hard for patients – every single GP across the land is in agreement with this.

Despite all of these pressures, the structure of the general practice model has not changed. GPs still have to see these more complex patients in ten minutes. Increasing the length of the appointment to fifteen minutes will mean longer surgeries in order to accommodate the same number of appointments, yet if we don't maintain the number of appointments then the demand will increase further. Each appointment needs writing up meticulously and referrals and paperwork take time that does not exist in the working day.

It gets worse. Increasing numbers of GPs are leaving the profession or retiring. New recruits are reluctant to work full time or commit to a single practice, citing workload pressures as the cause. The same is happening with practice nurses. A new breed of clinicians is being drafted in: physician associates, advanced practitioners and social prescribers, among others.

A GP takes ten years to train. That's five years at medical school and then a further five years of postgraduate training. I would argue it takes another five years to gain the experience needed to become a confident GP. That's a long time.

Things have changed with the global pandemic. Those of us who were resistant to using technology as part of patient consultations have had our hands forced. We were restricted by the coronavirus as to what we could see face-to-face, so traditional clinics were turned to phone calls and video consultations, and even the most die-hard critics realised that these worked well for both patient and clinician. This might herald a whole new way of working in general practice and it might even mean those doctors who were previously feeling the pressure of balancing work and family life could have the option of working from home.

Losing large numbers of our elderly and vulnerable patients, some of whom we had looked after for years, was heartbreaking and highlighted the inequalities found in healthcare even in the most developed countries.

Despite this, the overwhelming support we got as healthcare professionals from the public during one of our most testing times was incredible. When I came home from talking to those bereft relatives, seeing a rainbow in the window of a house lifted me up.

So why am I still an advocate for general practice as a profession? Sometimes I ask myself the same question. I work in a large inner-city practice; I am not immune to these pressures. I work full time, but despite this I find myself frequently logging in from home on evenings and weekends to keep afloat. But do I regret becoming a GP?

Absolutely not.

It is often said that general practice is an easy job to do badly and a hard job to do well.

When it is done well, true general practice can be a thing of beauty. There is still one element of the job that has not changed in all the years the profession has been around: the interaction between the patients and their doctor. When it is just me and a patient in a room talking about their health problem, and I am doing the job I choose to do, then it works.

Epilogue

I cannot pretend that there are not days when I look at my clinic list and feel a sense of impending doom, when I look down the names of patients on the list and the brief summary of their problem and shudder. But as soon as I start calling them in, that feeling starts to ebb away. Each time a patient says 'thank you' or asks me how I am, or remembers something I told them about myself previously, a warmer feeling takes its place. The satisfaction of getting a diagnosis right, the pride of seeing a patient get better because of something I did, still stands up against those pressures. Even the harder parts have their rewards – breaking bad news, supporting a patient through a bereavement or dealing with a new cancer diagnosis. These are the times I am reminded why I chose general practice; these are the times the doctor–patient relationship shines through the murky fog that can often seem impassable.

I have been a full-time GP for over ten years now and, although I still have much to learn, I feel I am entitled to an opinion about my profession.

To the patients I would say: value your GP. Don't take us for granted. The difficulty getting an appointment is not specific to your practice, and it is not the fault of your GP, who is working as hard as they possibly can. If you are kept waiting for your appointment, it is because the people before you have been exceptionally unwell. When we see you, we will always do our best for you. Be nice to the receptionists; they are only doing their job. It is not their fault if there are no appointments in the system. Over time, it is likely that you may see a clinician other than your GP for your medical problem and I have no doubt they too will do their best for you.

To the policymakers I would say: we need to be able to trust you, now more than ever. You are the people who can make a difference to our workload and the quality of care we give our patients. Be realistic, don't make false pledges. Promising thousands of extra GPs over a period of time will only set patients' expectations high and is almost always doomed to fail. The current system is not working. Throwing money at it is akin to putting a plaster over a severed limb. The pandemic has taught us that we can work in different ways and still have patients at the heart of healthcare. It needs an overhaul, but that overhaul must involve us GPs who are on the frontline every day. We arc the ones who understand the pressures more than anyone else. We are the ones who understand what changes need to be made. Work with us. We generally have the public on our side, so don't try to vilify us.

To my fellow GP colleagues I would say: think about why you came into this job to begin with. Try to hold on to that if you can. Yes, each day will come with its own set of challenges but it will also come with its own set of rewards. If the pressures are such that you are no longer enjoying the job and it is having an adverse effect on your health, then there is help available for doctors. Please seek it out. Otherwise, be realistic about the job but also champion its positive sides to the students and to the public. The old girl is in need of a boost.

I can honestly say that I still enjoy coming into work. I enjoy teaching my medical students; I love being a GP trainer and helping to mould our future workforce. I cannot overstate how much my friendships with my colleagues mean to me. My colleagues are my work family. No GP can work without their team, and this true for the whole of the NHS. It is each individual staff member who makes it what it is.

I enjoy all of these things, but most of all I enjoy getting it right for my patients.

Acknowledgements

This book has been such a cathartic experience to write, but I couldn't have done it without Alfred and Louise, who sat and listened to each chapter as I wrote it no matter what time of day or night it was. To Debbie and Chris for all their support, not just with the book but with everything leading up to it. Of course, all the amazing staff I work with. And, of course, to Mama Khan!